Taste of

TOTALITY

Disclaimer

We have used our best efforts in preparing this cookbook, and the information is provided solely as information. We make no representation or warranties with respect to the accuracy or completeness of the contents of this cookbook and we specifically disclaim any implied warranties of merchantability or fitness for any particular purpose.

All material in this cookbook is provided for your information only and may not be construed as medical advice or instruction. No action or inaction should be taken based solely on the contents of this information; instead, readers should consult appropriate health professionals on any matter relating to their health and well-being.

WE DO NOT CLAIM TO BE DOCTORS OR REGISTERED DIETITIANS. THE INFORMATION IN THIS BOOK IS MERELY OUR PERSONAL OPINION AND DOES NOT REPLACE PROFESSIONAL MEDICAL OR NUTRITIONAL ADVICE.

Use your best judgment and proper discretion when preparing or consuming any food.

Forward from Chef Greg J. Eisele

C.E.C / PC-II, Culinary Program Director, University of Tennessee and President of the American Culinary Federation's Smoky Mountain Chapter

Michelle Williams's passion for nutritional balance, good health, and healthy education has few equals. I clearly realized this when she totally captivated a crowd of young teenagers, at 9:00am, on a Monday morning by tossing them apples and dancing to rap music. I normally demand this type of consideration; however, mine comes from a tall chef hat, clipboard, reading glasses and a grimace.

Our initial meeting was a team interview for a well-known local magazine, and we both found that we had very similar philosophies when it came to all things food and culinary.

Michelle asked during the interview what my favorite dish was and I replied, "It's a dish crusted in enthusiasm and sautéd with passion." I could see the spark in her eye and knew we would be partners in our culinary worlds. After this connection, Michelle joined our local American Culinary Federation Chapter as a professional member. At her first meeting, she surprised all of our senior chefs. The theme du jour was "Gluten-free" with a workshop and group menu planning competition. Michelle and her

5

husband, Scott, lead their team to win 1st place AND THEY WON BY A LANDSLIDE! I later found out that the senior chefs did not have any input in the menu planning. It was all Michelle and Scott!

As time continued, we have worked on various mutual projects: Instruction and teaching in the UT Culinary Program, American Culinary Federation Chef and Child programs, local TV segments, a Bacon Fest charity event and more.

I am truly honored to partner with Michelle, Scott and the entire Totality Living Well Team!

About Greg:
Master Chef Greg Eisele began his culinary career on a New Year's Eve as a busboy in the award winning Seventh Inn Restaurant in St. Louis. From there he rapidly moved from the dining room staff to the kitchen team. After two short years, he was promoted to Sous Chef, then Executive Sous Chef of this 4 Star restaurant and spent 8 years in that position. While serving under Chef Martin George C.E.C., they earned a 4 Star (Mobile Rating) for Culinary Excellence in 1990. Recognizing the need for professional education, Chef Eisele graduated at Forrest Park via the American Culinary Federation and completed a Pastry Chef internship at the Adams Mark hotel.

He was recruited out of the retail restaurant business by ARAMARK Corporation (The world's largest provider of contract culinary services) as a District Executive Chef for St.Louis, Nashville, and the Knoxville marketplace. Lasting 25 years, his responsibilities included competition coordinator and coach for the southern region, upscale catering events for up to 30,000 and had over 25 chefs reporting to him.

For the past 10 years, he has been a Regional Executive Chef and senior manager, trainer and Executive chef with ARAMARK at the University of Tennessee. His achievements in training and competition led to his selection to lead UT's Culinary Program. His passion for the industry drove peers to elect him as President of the local chapter of the American Culinary Federation.

In addition to training and managing culinary professionals, Chef Eisele brings the science and skills of cooking to the general public through UT's non-credit cooking classes and TV culinary segments on local and regional stations. Chef Eisele has earned an extensive number of certifications and awards on the local, regional and national levels.

Forward from Nathan Sparks

Publisher and Editor of Cityview Magazine

At the age of 57 I found myself looking at the biometric scale in disbelief. There was just no way I could have 34% body fat. Sadly, I had fallen prey to the businessman's sedentary lifestyle complete with poor diet and inadequate exercise. The answer to my prayers for a new and healthy lifestyle came in the form of Scott and Michelle Williams. Although I knew that this change was something I desperately needed, my enthusiasm was somewhat similar to a child being told to clean his room.

One of the first things Scott said to me was, "You are going to have a difficult time eating enough." The very thought made me laugh and cringe all in the same breath. Visions of mountains of tasteless food filled my imagination, but this was not to be. The diet plan I got was filled with wonderful foods and creative ways to prepare them all in a super healthy manner. To my further surprise, healthy didn't mean bland.

Coupled with a very realistic exercise plan working with Scott, their advice got me back on track. My body fat dropped to 20%, my muscle mass increased and my level of happiness soared! I hope you will

find preparing these recipes as satisfying for you and your family as I have. Scott and Michelle have solved the riddle of how to eat healthy and still enjoy a gourmet taste experience. Bravo!

About Nathan: Nathan Sparks is the publisher and Editor of Cityview Magazine and a former owner and chef of a small French Bistro. His love for food lies only second to his love for adventure.

Acknowledgements

The Taste of Totality, a Jumpstart to the Ultimate Level of Health would never have happened without inspiration from our clients and the talented team of people who believed enough in our mission to join in and help make this possible. The first contributor we would like to thank is staff member, Jesse Johnson. Jesse shares our passion for health and wellness and good food! He shared some unique dishes for this book and we are certain that you will enjoy trying them for yourself.

We also extend a warm note of appreciation to friend, mentor and colleague, Chef Greg Eisele for being such a huge support both in the kitchen and out and to his exceptional culinary staff at the UT Culinary Department who took the time to create some exquisite recipes for this book. Thank you to Eric and JC Muffett, owners of Zi Olive - Knoxville, for helping us narrow down the the unthinkable combinations of their delicious oils and balsamics by creating some extra special marinades and vinaigrettes for our readers.

We thank client and friend Kathy Clare for talking incessantly about the need for a cookbook before, during and after our training sessions, and then organizing recipes and urging us to do our first food photography shoot at her house. She hosted, organized, styled food, cooked, cleaned and smiled the whole time and was instrumental in launching this tiring, day-long, kick-off project. To Francis Bisek, our amazing client who allowed us to be a part of his health journey as he radically transformed his health over a 14 month period and then stepped up with patience and skill to help us put this book together when we didn't have a clue. Frank, thank you for being a special part of this milestone journey and for helping make this possible! We are honored to call you friend as well. To our super talented photographers, Colby McLemore and Elizabeth Myers, we appreciate you both for taking our food and creating amazing pictures in the home and even on our back porch! A special word of thanks to Nathan Sparks, Publisher of Cityview Magazine, client and friend, for showcasing our work in his publication so that we could share our mission of health and for supporting us behind the scenes as we worked to create this piece. We aren't legal experts and sincerely appreciate the guidance of our attorney and friend, Keith Stewart in business and in the development of this book. We want to thank our children for their never-ending patience as we tested, created, triumphed, failed and pursued with fatigue with their encouraging and understanding dispositions. Last, but certainly not least, we thank our clients who make our business possible. They were and are the key source of inspiration for us sharing our recipes and who have been so understanding when we've needed to reschedule our time with them to put this project before them.

This book is dedicated to
Aaron Kelly and Andrew Kelly...

....two amazing sons who have patiently supported our efforts in teaching them and our community healthy living principles. They have graciously celebrated our successful dishes with us, endured our accidental culinary disasters with grace and supported us through it all with encouragement and respect. It has been quite enjoyable observing them apply the balance of our clean eating principles along with moderation with more popular decadent foods in their daily choices as they grow into young men.

We also dedicate this book to
our wonderful clients, ...

... who were over the past few years, the inspiration for writing this book through their questions and desire for a variety of dishes as they journeyed with our guidance to living a healthier lifestyle. We are grateful to them all for pushing us to reaching a milestone that we may have not otherwise sought out to do.

The Taste of Totality Mindset

"There are so many health nuts out there who eat nothing but natural foods but they don't exercise and they look terrible. Then there are other people who exercise like a son-of-a-gun but eat a lot of junk... Exercise is king. Nutrition is queen. Put them together and you've got a kingdom."

~ Jack LaLanne, American fitness, exercise and nutritional expert and motivational speaker

"My philosophy to food and healthy eating has always been about enjoying everything in a balanced and sane way. Food is one of life's greatest joys yet we've reached this really sad point where we're turning food into the enemy, and something to be afraid of. I believe that when you use good ingredients to make pasta dishes, salads, stews, burgers, grilled vegetables, fruit salads, and even outrageous cakes, they all have a place in our diets. We just need to rediscover our common sense: if you want to curl up and eat macaroni and cheese every once in a while - that's alright! Just have a sensible portion next to a fresh salad, and don't eat a big old helping of chocolate cake afterwards."

~ Jamie Oliver, Celebrity food chef, author and founder of the Food Revolution Campaign

"If I could encourage individuals to make just one dietary change, it would be to eliminate sugary foods - including corn starch, high-fructose corn sweetener, maltodextrin, and others - from their diet. Sadly, companies load aisles in the supermarket with foods that may be fine when consumed in moderation, but can quickly add extra empty calories to your diet and leave you wanting more, leading to weight gain and swinging energy levels."

~ Arnold Schwarzenegger, Multiple Mr. Olympia champion, former Governor of California and former Chairman of the President's Council on Physical Fitness and Sports

Taste of Totality Testimonials

"Health begins and ends with what you eat! Michelle and Scott understand this. They are awesome. This book will be one of the best things you will read this year and for many years."

Tom Rogers MD
Performance Medicine
Johnson City, TN / Kingsport, TN / Knoxville, TN

"In more than a decade, I have seen Michelle and Scott create a powerful team to demonstrate their dedication to health ∞ wellbeing for families ∞ the community as a whole. Their new Cookbook is only a piece of their continued contribution to lift people to a new level of health and wellbeing."

Mardell Hill
Author of Intestinal Health - A Practical Guide to Complete Abdominal Comfort
www.IntestinalHealthBook.com
Boulder, CO

"I have recently had the pleasure of getting to know Michelle and Scott on a personal and professional level. I could not be more proud of what they have done in this community, and what I know they are going to continue to do! They are not only a powerhouse duo in the personal training arena, but also compassionate health coaches that have an entirely different, refreshing approach to everything mind, body, and spirit. They are a unique asset to the uprising of the healthy and holistic lifestyle choices in Knoxville. Everyone they touch would certainly agree. The sky's the limit for these two, and they share that love and optimistic compassion in every explicit detail of their work. This book will be a tremendous asset to anyone seeking healthy food that is delicious for once, and easy to make! I believe in their vision, and know that like everything else they set out to do, this book will be nothing short of perfection. "

Shane Archer
Owner - Grow Knoxville Salon
Knoxville, TN

"Scott and Michelle have been coming on 10News at Noon for 3 years now to share their recipes. So glad to see them putting them all in one place! They always have fun, tasty, creative, and most of all, healthy, recipes that the viewers and I love!"

Mary Scott
TV News Anchor
Knoxville, TN

Scott and Michelle Williams combine many years of practical experience with intense formal training in health and wellness. They have developed a total health program that is unrivaled in our area.

Matt Poteet
CEO/ Owner
Compounding Pharmacy of America
Knoxville, TN

"BEING INFLUENCED BY MICHELLE'S NUTRITION AND HEALTH IDEAS HAS INSPIRED ME TO TRY NEW THINGS. BECAUSE OF HER, I NOW REGULARLY USE COCONUT OIL, EAT AND LOVE KALE, AND USE THE AMINO ACID, L-THEANINE. HER KNOWLEDGE AND PASSION FOR NATURAL HEALTH IS CONTAGIOUS!"

Alisa King
Teacher
Denver, CO

"When I first met Michelle I was a mid-40's, ex-competitive runner with a poor diet, overweight, with chronic heartburn which I treated with prescription drugs (proton pump inhibitors).

Michelle had just begun her journey into nutrition and physical training.

Based on a question I had asked about nutrition, and the effects of these drugs on my overall health I decided to take a hard look at my life and my health. My first big step was incorporating coconut oil into my diet which alleviated my heartburn symptoms. After a month I was able to discontinue the PPI's that I had been consuming for over 4 years.

Life is good...."

G. Wrap
CEO Software
San Francisco, CA

15

"Working with Scott and Michelle in the gym and the kitchen added tremendous value to my life. They understand health and fitness at a level that is extraordinary. Scott and Michelle taught me how to shop for real food and how to use real food to make healthy recipes that are full of flavor. Their mantra of "eating clean" works miracles."

Keith D. Stewart
Lawyer
Knoxville, TN

"MY EXPERIENCE WITH TOTALITY LIVING WELL WAS A FANTASTIC ONE. SCOTT DEVELOPED BOTH FITNESS AND NUTRITION PLANS THAT WORKED FOR MY LIFESTYLE AND BODY TYPE. I HAD BEEN LOOKING FOR SOMEONE THAT COULD TRULY HELP ME GET THE RESULTS I WAS LOOKING FOR. HE HELPED ME GET ON THE RIGHT PATH TO ACCOMPLISH THE GOALS THAT I HAD SET OUT FOR MYSELF. I LEARNED THAT EATING NUTRITIOUS MEALS AND WORKING OUT PROPERLY IS INCREDIBLY IMPORTANT AND MAKES A HUGE DIFFERENCE IN YOUR EVERYDAY LIFE. AS A RESULT, I FELT BETTER AND WAS SEEING MY BODY CHANGE. EVEN THOUGH I'VE MOVED AWAY FROM KNOXVILLE, I'VE KEPT PURSUING MY GOALS WITH THE TECHNIQUES THEY'VE TAUGHT ME. ON TOP OF ALL THAT, I MADE SOME NEW FRIENDS IN THE PROCESS. SCOTT AND MICHELLE RUN AN INCREDIBLE PROGRAM."

Cameron Taylor
Anchor/Reporter
Chattanooga, TN

"Scott and Michelle are an amazing couple! They are each devoted to overall health and wellness, and together they provide the perfect balance in coaching. I admire them individually and together and trust them for guidance in all areas of my life. I consider it a blessing to know them!"

Angela Russo
Kokomo, IN

"I have known Scott Williams for 20 years and ever since the first day we met he was always excited by health, fitness and especially cooking. It is nice to see Scott live out his passion. Now that he's teamed up with his wife Michelle, they are a perfect combo. They are a win-win duo in this endeavor!!"

Rick Sosias
Owner of Fit Foods 4U
Denver, CO

"Scott has taught me to eat with spiritual integrity. Everything contains energy and ensuring that positive energy nourishes my body. Positive energy foods are: humanely raised and processed meats, organic fruits and vegetables which are grown and harvested by fair labor."

Brian Fun
Massage Therapist
Denver, Colorado

"The impact that Scott and Michelle have on the lives and health of our patients, as well as us personally, is tremendous. Their passion, through Totality, for true wellness of mind and body is inspiring, and all of us could stand a dose of that."

Michael Fields MD
Anya Zerilla NP
Fields Center for Women's Health and Robotic Surgery
Knoxville, TN

"Michelle and Scott Williams have an incredible passion for health that helps bring the Knoxville community together"

Eddie Reymond
Owner - Eddie's Health Shoppe
Knoxville, TN

"Scott and Michelle changed my life! I only thought I had been eating the right foods. They taught me all about eating "clean" and portion control. Their passion for proper nutrition and exercising energizes clients like me. Working out and eating right are not difficult the way they teach and inspire. They actually make it fun!"

Martha Dooley
Director of Media Relations, Knox Co. Sheriff's Office
Knoxville, TN

"Michelle and Scott represent the true meaning of personal trainer and personal coach. Their unprecedented dedication, and "laser" focus they give to their clients excels them to the highest level of professionalism in the health & wellness industry. Both of them need to get ready for an uncommon promotion in a way that they would have never dreamed. I'm gleaming with happiness knowing I'm a Totality Woman Transformed!!!"

Andrea Clowers
Marketing Representative
Knoxville, TN

"Before working with Scott Williams and Totality Living Well, my workouts were infrequent and unscripted. If I did make it to the gym, I didn't get there with any sense of what I should be doing. Working with Scott changed all of that. Every workout had a purpose, and there were always goals in mind. He made it so that when I now walk into a gym, I can confidently look around, and know what I should be doing, and why.

I saw immediate changes and results while working with Scott, but more importantly, I have been able to maintain those physical and nutritional changes beyond our time together.

Just as important as all of that, Scott was fantastic to work with. He has a great way of being able to connect with his clients, while also pushing you to do your best. Working with Totality Living Well was a life-changing experience that I'll always be grateful to have made."

Nick Carboni
Sports Anchor
Charlotte, NC

"Michelle is a joy to work with! I came to her ready to make a change but nervous to put myself out "there". She gave me the tools, the knowledge, and support I needed to change my life for the better. I highly recommend her to any woman out there looking to better herself physically and mentally. She's amazing!!"

Crystal Shelton
Knoxville, TN

"I came to Totality looking to change my exercise routine up to see what my body was capable of...I've seen wonderful results. The nutrition guidance has been worth the experience alone..."

Steve Shelton
Knoxville, TN

"Greetings! I have known Michelle Williams for more than 15 years. Even that far back, Michelle was extremely health conscious and driven to find more natural ways to eat and live, so her family could live a healthier life. Health, exercise and nutrition are passions in her life, not only for her to become better and look younger, but to help all of us accomplish the same. It is too easy to sit back and let the weight accumulate and chalk it up to age... fortunately Michelle is not content with that position in life. She is here to be helpful and to guide us into being our best at any age. THANKS MICHELLE!!!"

Jenine Holtz Dobie
Limu Promoter, Jenine.iamlimu.com
Colorado Springs, Colorado

"Scott & Michelle Williams offer the whole health package: physical, emotional, nutritional and environmental. I cannot thank them enough for getting me back into the gym after years of leading a sedentary lifestyle. If there is hope for me, there's hope for everyone. Regardless of where you are in your wellness goals, it's never too late to start. Scott & Michelle are remarkable. They are well educated, hard working and they truly care about every single client."

Wendy Blackburn
Insurance broker
Knoxville, TN

"Until last year, I had always said I didn't have time to do a lot of meal prep. That changed when Michelle and Scott introduced me to easy, delicious recipes that my husband Steve and I could prepare and enjoy together. It's such a joy to sit down to a beautiful, colorful meal after an intense workout. This isn't a diet, it's all about a lifestyle reboot."

Lori Tucker
TV News Anchor
Knoxville, TN

"With 15 years in the medical field we have met a lot of fitness trainers and people in nutrition. Scott and Michelle are health coaches. With Totality Living Well people get a TOTAL transformation. Scott and Michelle focus on the whole person by recognizing mind, body and spirit. The thing that sets them apart is their intuition and knowledge of the individuals who live in the real world. Their nutritional principles just make sense and are easy to apply. We highly recommend them to all and Totality is exactly what Knoxville needs...a Total transformation!"

Timothy and Amber Fox
Owners / Medical Practitioners
Fountain of Youth Medical
Knoxville, TN

Taste of Totality, a Jumpstart to the Ultimate Level of Health

What an exciting journey it has been creating our first cookbook together, Taste of Totality, a Jumpstart to the Ultimate Level of Health. After years of individually pursuing a special interest in nutrition, fitness and lifestyle balance, this book includes many of the personal philosophies that we have each adopted (and share) through the years as we have sought out to learn in our own health journeys. With a cumulative 40 years of experience in serving and sharing with others in the arena of fitness, nutrition and wellness education, it is a true honor to now share those views with you, our readers.

As children we were each influenced by adults who had a lasting impact on our lives and who were monumental in shaping our thoughts when it came to healthy living.

Having spent summers with a grandfather who had a passion for gardening and cultivating produce, learning the value of growing and harvesting organically grown food (Michelle), and meeting Jack LaLanne and Arnold Schwarzenegger (Scott) who both shared the importance of avoiding processed food and the gift we give ourselves in quality movement of the body, we saw at young ages that health is to be taken seriously. From boycotting lunch food in elementary school because nobody could give the sugar content (Michelle), to learning to read labels and include only pure foods as a lifestyle (Scott), we were each laying the groundwork for what we do today.

Shortly after meeting one another in 2013, we began our company, Totality Living Well, with a mutual passion for bringing health and wellness awareness to those in our community of Knoxville, Tennessee with clean eating principles and movement of the body through personal balance of body, mindset and spirit. Around that same time we began a monthly healthy cooking segment on our local NBC affiliate, WBIR-TV. These monthly segments usually snuck up on us and we sometimes had to rally to create something that we thought viewers would enjoy. Many of those recipes have been included in this book. At other times during our frantic schedules of training clients, chauffeuring kids to and from school, sports, friends and appointments, working with coaching clients and trying to grow our business with various meetings and projects, we found ourselves trying to figure out how we were going to create a healthy, balanced family meal with minimal items in the house. Those moments led to some of our most creative recipes! See our Peach-Basil Salad and Teriyaki Marinated Pork Tenderloin. We ended up showing that on WBIR too!

You may notice turtles in the photos throughout the book. Each turtle has a message. "Be Strong," "Believe," "Laugh out Loud" and "Life is a Journey." Three of those turtles were collected at a time during life change of relocating and rebuilding (Michelle and the two boys). Each turtle served as individual mantras and as a joint family mantra to keep moving forward regardless of life's challenges. After marrying, we came across another turtle with another message: "Life is a Journey." It is the smallest turtle, but not insignificant. We have now combined them all to create a unified mantra, "Be strong, believe, and laugh out loud. Life is a journey." It serves as a daily reminder to keep going with balance no matter what obstacle lies in our path.

As health coaches we have noticed that people generally experience an imbalance of sorts with food. People being concerned with eating too much, gaining weight, losing weight, eating too little, avoiding certain food groups altogether, starving, dieting, trying to overcome food sensitivities, self-soothing with an unusually high amount of decadent treats, comparing themselves to someone with a naturally higher metabolism or a different genetic disposition....the list goes on. Some of the most common challenges we have seen our clients face is lack of variety, a misconception that heathier foods have to be bland and boring and that cooking is overly complicated. While we genuinely appreciate beautiful culinary cuisine and enjoy special decadent treats in moderation, we also understand the importance of balance. As an instructor of healthy cooking at the University of Tennessee Culinary Department (Michelle), friend and UT Culinary Director, Master Chef Greg Eisele and some select culinary students have graciously volunteered a few recipes for this book that have more of a culinary flair with our Totality influence. We have aimed to create a variety of interesting dishes that are healthy, relatively simple and loaded with flavor.

As you comb through the recipes, we hope that you feel inspired to try them. As you see the turtles, we encourage you to remember that eating can be about balance: having the strength of discipline, believing in the process of finding balance and believing in yourself along the way, enjoying the fun moments with special treats, laughter and always being mindful that life is a journey. Eating doesn't have to be all or nothing. Strive for a healthy balance and ENJOY the process!

We have seen our clients experience some of their biggest changes in health for the better when they relax a bit and enjoy a smorgasbord of foods that are generally clean while allowing special moments for treats. Our book includes some super healthy, super clean dishes, but also allows for treat foods to enjoy in moderation. We want to encourage our readers to explore some of our clean substitutes and to try them in your pantry and to incorporate them in your routine and see what positive changes that you might experience.

If you don't have all of the ingredients that a recipe calls for, change it up and use what you have. You never know if it will be the next big hit for your family or that dinner party with your friends. We like to have fun with our food. Sometimes some of the most unconventional pairings can be your most successful meals. We've had many one-hit wonder meals because of that very thing. We've also had some pretty big mishaps that we have all laughed about. Once our kids were given French toast accidentally sprinkled with cumin instead of cinnamon (Michelle). It was quickly dubbed as Mexican French Toast and the kids gave it an honest try. It wasn't a hit, but it created a fun memory that is surely NOT to be recreated, and we all got a good laugh from it!

Our book isn't just about recipes. We have included food tips that have meant something to us as certified nutrition specialists helping our clients over the years. We believe that food free of processed ingredients and artificial sweeteners and foods that are closest to their natural states are useful for the body and help lead to better health. We sincerely hope you enjoy trying some new things as you journey!

In great health,

Scott and Michelle Williams

Totality Living Well

23

Table of Contents

Oven Creations   79

Stove Top Wonders   103

Grilling Cuisine 145

Culinary Creations by the UT Culinary Department   165

The Totality Philosophy

When we set out to make this book, we knew that we wanted to include recipes which reflect the principles and philosophies that have worked for us and the numerous clients we have coached in health. We view health as being a comprehensive balance of the body, mindset and spirit. When it comes to the body, fitness and nutrition go together. We are frequently asked about which foods we avoid. The short answer is that we enjoy all food. It provides energy for the body and sustains life. It is the nucleus of most cultural events - weddings, celebrations, holidays, births, deaths, reunions and farewell departures. It can be elaborate and artistic or simple and serve as a means of survival. Basically, food is a big deal no matter how you look at it. While it was important for us to create healthy recipes, we also wanted our readers to enjoy flavor and to have dishes that could be utilized in a variety of settings. We wanted you to have fun with healthy food!

We embrace specific foods for their health benefits and are always eager to learn why so many are touted for being either good or bad. Our stance is that all food has a place in the human diet as long as moderation, variety and purity are part of the equation. Is can be confusing when a random food is suddenly thrown into the limelight and promoted as the new wonder food to end all of your health problems, then is discredited with a study two years later. Our stance to all of the superfoods that are out there is that moderation is still the key and is not the only tool in the toolbox of health.

We recognize that dietary needs vary greatly by the individual. While we provide customized nutrition plans and guidelines for each of our clients as professionals certified in nutrition, we want to remind our readers that this book is not intended to serve as a meal plan, weight loss/weight goal guideline or to fix health ailments. Recipes which include items that are known allergens or trigger sensitivities should be substituted or avoided. As always, contact your medical professional if you have questions or concerns about your health.

Our Totality Gems section contains some information that we believe is vital to a healthier you as you incorporate some of our recipes. We personally feel that some of these basic gems can serve as building blocks to healthier habits. We encourage you to try one or all as you journey through in your Taste of Totality.

Unlike the majority of other cookbooks, we have decided to divide our recipes by cooking method categories: No Bake Simplicity, Stove Top Wonders, Oven Creations and Grilling Cuisine. A bonus category includes a list of three specialty dishes created by our friends at the UT Culinary Department under the direction of Chef Greg Eisele. These dishes incorporate the Totality principles with a bit more culinary flair. We encourage you to try them!

For anyone who likes to crunch numbers, we have decided to include a macronutrient breakdown of our recipes. The majority of our recipes can be consumed regularly as part of a health-conscious lifestyle. You will also find a few treats along the way.

Have fun. Get creative and keep an open mind. Don't be apprehensive in switching up the ingredients when you need to substitute or feel inspired to add an ingredient or two! Now let's get started and remember,

"A recipe has no soul. YOU as the cook must bring soul to the recipe." - Thomas Keller

Totality Gems

We call these little tips, observations and foods our Totality Gems. We are sharing these with you because we have seen some interesting things happen after learning about them, incorporating them into our personal health journeys and then observing our many clients who have success stories of their own after utilizing them. Feel free to consider them in your own plan.

Coconut Oil

Coconut oil and the health benefits that can occur when used in moderation have been impressive with our observations. It is higher in saturated fats, and like other oils, shouldn't be consumed in large quantities. At most, 2 tablespoons per day is plenty. We like it because of its molecular structure being a medium-chain triglyceride. In the 1980's, US pig farmers wanted to fatten their livestock and gave them a diet containing coconut oil. They began to notice that the pigs were losing weight. They later learned that the molecular structure had something to do with it. The human body knows exactly what to do with this type of molecular structure because human breast milk is a medium-chain triglyceride. Coconut oil is a fat that helps to burn fat and aids in fighting viral, bacterial and fungal infections. If you are new to coconut oil, try it with scrambled eggs or sauteeing some vegetables with just a teaspoon of the oil. Organic Extra Virgin Unrefined Coconut Oil is what we use and recommend to our clients. We also have it in our first aid kit.

We enjoy other oils too and do not advocate coconut oil as the only oil to be utilized in a healthy lifestyle. If you would like to read more about Coconut Oil and its benefits you can check out the many coconut oil books written by Dr. Bruce Fife.

Water

Water is essential to life and to helping the human body at a cellular level. A large number of Americans don't drink enough water. We have seen national statistics matched repeatedly on our smaller client level. Our recommendations to clients is to drink at least half of their body weight in ounces for a daily minimum amount before accounting for any sort of exercise. Adding lemon, lime or another fruit can help the palate to acclimate to water. Because the salivary glands aid with the first step of digestion, we recommend that small sips of room temperature water be taken with food. The temperature of the water allows the salivary enzymes to break down the food more effectively. We recommend consuming ice cold water during other times of water intake to assist the body in helping to rev the body's metabolism. While ice cold water plays a small role in helping the metabolism and so much more needs to occur to effectively speed up the metabolism, all small things can add up!

When the body is dehydrated, it can actually send a hunger signal to the brain. When the body is adequately hydrated, hunger often diminishes. To learn more about the importance of hydration, check out *Your Body's Many Cries for Water* by Fereydoon Batmanghelidj. There is an abundant amount of scientific evidence on the signs of dehydration in this book.

Frequency of Eating

We often see that most people undereat and think that a state of hunger is not an issue. In our own personal experience working with clients, adequate caloric needs must be met to keep the metabolism burning and to maintain muscle mass.

We have seen great benefits when frequent food intake is implemented with 5 meals per day. Three larger meals (typically known as breakfast, lunch and dinner) and two small meals per day (that many would refer to as a snack).

Portion Sizes

Portion size continues to be a topic of question with our clients when we first begin to work with them with the issue being either too little or too much in one meal sitting. There are many portion guides available today. One is produced by the U.S. Government at www.ChooseMyPlate.gov. You can reference that website as a source for proper eating if you are uncertain about your portion sizes. On a more practical level, we share the simple concept of using your hands as your measuring tools. Primitive man had to use hands as a bowl. In most cases, the amount that your two hands can hold at one sitting will correspond to the amount that your stomach can hold. One exception would be with someone who has had their stomach size altered through surgery. Another way to gauge a personal portion size is to cup both of your hands over your plate in a mound when you are served food at a restaurant. Restaurant portion sizes are often very generous and this can help you to determine if some of your food needs to be taken home and saved for another meal. When it comes to smaller meals like snacks, the size of your fist is a good guideline to follow. When you begin to look at portion sizes in this manner, you can get a better idea of how much you are putting into your body in a single meal.

Chew Your Food!

Chances are you have been reminded of the importance of chewing your food by either a parent or grandparent at some point in your life. As previously mentioned, chewing food is very important on a variety of levels. The digestion process begins with chewing the food as it allows enzymes to break down the food secreted by the salivary glands. Food needs to be chewed until it has turned soft enough to swallow without having to wash it down with a ton of liquid. That usually means that bites need to be smaller. One of the worst things we can do is to eat large bites in a rush. The stomach and brain communicate as food is taken into the body. It takes a while for the brain to realize that the stomach is full. The brain sends messages to the body to secreting hormones called leptin and ghrelin. Ghrelin is the hormone that tells us to eat. Leptin is the hormone that tells us to stop. If you have eaten reasonable portion sizes, are adequately hydrated and still feel hungry, wait for 20 minutes for the brain to get the message from the stomach that it is full. It is important that you wait this entire 20 minutes for the "snail mail" to be delivered to the brain. You can buy time by adding a very small second portion to your plate and conversing with those around you. Try it. You might be surprised that you suddenly don't feel hungry anymore.

Himalayan Pink Salt

Iodized salt and sea salt are two common types of salt that we have as options in restaurants and in the grocery stores. You may have also seen Kosher salt in these places. Salt is an important component in the foods we eat and in our health in general. It livens up the flavor of our foods and traps calcium and other vital nutrients in the body. The kidneys use it for electrolyte distribution and it is an important component of blood pressure. It protects us from heat-related problems like strokes. Too much salt can be a problem too.

We prefer sea salt above iodized salt and Himalayan pink salt above sea salt for its health benefits. Himalayan pink salt has over 84 trace minerals that can benefit the human body. Even though this is a prehistoric crystal, it is just now becoming known for all of its benefits from dietary to environmental. Himalayan salt blocks are available to cook on and they mildly season the foods prepared on them. We asked the UT Culinary Department to create a dish on a salt block for us. Check out the Herb Seared Scallop recipe. It's fabulous.

Often called the "Gem of the mountains," this salt can be use in cooking with either coarse or fine granules. Like anything else, it has its place and is to be used in moderation. We like this salt for the milder flavor and for knowing that it has a healthy component. The general consensus among the clients we have introduced to Himalayan pink salt is that they love it. It doesn't really matter which salt you use but we encourage you to give this one a try!

The Spices of Life

Spices are other creative culinary art tools that anyone can add to simple dishes to make them lively. Spices were once used in older countries because the meats weren't as fresh and the smells and flavors of the not-so-fresh meats needed to be enhanced. If you do a bit of searching, you'll notice that different spices originated in different regions. While pairing traditional regional spices with certain foods is great in creating dishes, don't be afraid to step outside of the box.

Like herbs, spices can have a variety health benefits. Did you know that cinnamon is an effective anti-viral? Turmeric is a known as an anti-inflammatory and cayenne has been praised for its metabolic boosting properties. We break the rules all the time and cook with what feels right to us. Know that you are doing your body and your food a favor when you play around with spices.

Herbs with Benefits

We love herbs. They provide a variety of flavor and contain nutrients to enrich our food. They can make the most simple dishes extraordinary. There is nothing like working with fresh herbs. We have them growing indoors next to our kitchen sink and window. They are easy to grow, easy to cut and add to dishes. If you don't have access to fresh herbs, you can find a great assortment of dried herbs at your local supermarket. We also have a wide assortment of dried herbs in the cabinet next to our stove.

If you are not sure which herbs go in which dish, just smell them and decide for yourself. To activate the fragrance of fresh herbs, just rub them with your hands and the scent will be released onto your hands. They can be incorporated into a salad, sauteed, grilled, baked into a dish or simply added as a fresh garnish. It's hard to go wrong with cilantro, rosemary, basil varieties, thyme, sage, parsley, oregano, dill and mint. You can even tear them fresh and add them to whatever you are cooking and it will make a difference in your food. Don't overthink the herbs. If certain herbs smell good to you with what you are cooking, they will most likely work. Herbs give you the freedom of being a culinary artist in your own kitchen.

All Food Groups are Beneficial

We know from our training and experience that individual needs vary with dietary, nutrient, textural and biological needs. Sometimes those food choices are impacted by religious, political or even personal preferences. What is right for one isn't necessarily good for another. Aside from these exceptions, we personally embrace the idea that all food groups can be useful when it comes to overall health and wellness. It may sometimes be necessary for certain individuals to cut back, or even eliminate certain foods according to individual needs, yet we feel that all food groups can play an acceptable role in daily life for many people.

Medical testing is available to help those who suspect that they may have food allergies or sensitivities and can be very helpful in the often frustrating quest of pinpointing ailments. Please note that it isn't always necessary to subject yourself to food testing. We encourage you to listen to your body and to observe how certain foods make you feel first. If you suspect that certain foods may be a culprit in your health, you can contact a licensed medical professional, dietician or an experienced health professional.

What are Macros?

There is much talk in the nutrition and fitness realm about macros in nutrition. What does it all mean? In a nutshell, macros are macronutrients and those consist of three things: proteins, fats and carbohydrates. All of these components play a huge role in the health of the human body. Some people believe that some of the macronutrients need to be eliminated altogether, but our professional opinion is that all macronutrients are beneficial to the human body. We also agree that the ratio of those macronutrients are highly individualized. While one person may do extremely well with a higher amount of fats, others may benefit with a moderate balance of all three.

You can best determine your recommended macronutrient ratio by consulting a licensed or certified professional in nutrition. This is one of the things that we help our clients determine through testing and consulting. If you are currently tracking your macronutrient count, you may find it helpful that we have included the macro breakdown with each of our recipes.

Omega Fatty Acids

In our daily practice with clients, we continually see a regular pattern. People are often afraid to consume healthy fats. We understand the dilemma. If you feel that you have too much fat on your body to begin with and all you've ever read or heard tells you that fats are bad, why would you want to consume them? The truth is that the right fats can be good for you in overall health. The omegas are classified as omega-3, omega-6 and omega-9 fatty acids. The omega-3 and omega-6 fatty acids are "essential", meaning that the human body needs them and cannot produce them. Healthy essential omegas enhance moods, help regulate hormonal function and are beneficial for the hair and skin. Some beneficial omegas that we advocate include cold water high fat fish such salmon, avocados, olives, olive oil and a variety of seeds and nuts.

We learned much of our information on the subject directly from Dr. Udo Erasmus, an international authority on fats, oils, cholesterol in human health and on the specific breakdown of the omega fats during an extensive interview with him fifteen years ago (Michelle). To learn more about his research of the omega fatty acids, his book *Fats that Kill, Fats that Heal* is an exceptional book on the subject.

Don't Fear Your Carbs

Another macronutrient that gets a bad wrap is carbohydrates. Carbohydrates are an essential energy source. Your body needs them on a cellular level for organ function, intestinal health and water elimination. Having said that, not all carbs are created equal. The different types consist of simple and complex. Simple carbs are sugars and starches. They burn through the body quickly. Complex carbs are high in fiber, often high in vitamins and minerals and are usually found in whole plant foods and take longer for the body to break down.

 A lifestyle low in simple carbohydrates and higher in complex carbohydrates creates a healthier balance for the body. Some of our clients are pleasantly surprised when they experience favorable change after incorporating complex carbs that they once eliminated completely. Other clients who have eaten nothing but a diet of carbs enjoy greater health after learning to have proper balance of all macronutrients. There is a general tendency to over-consume carbohydrates in either form, so again, moderation and balance are key.   A licensed or certified nutrition expert can assist individuals seeking individualized guidance on carbohydrate intake.

Importance of Protein

Protein is is an important building block in your body. Your body needs it to repair tissues and for enzyme and hormone function. Our bones, muscles, skin and blood require it because protein is an important building block for them. We frequently see people undereat and under consume an adequate amount of protein to sustain their health. When our clients begin to balance out out their macronutrients, including the adequate intake of protein, the body responds favorably. Opinions about protein ratios vary among experts in nutrition, so consult with someone you trust who is licensed or certified if you have questions about your own protein intake.

Artificial Sweeteners

In our opinion, some of the most detrimental substances on the market today are the artificial sweeteners that have been introduced into the American food supply. We have seen the improvements made in both physical and cognitive health after helping clients wean from artificial sweeteners. After speaking with medical professionals and drawing our own conclusions based on research, we are convinced that the human body does not know how to adequately break down and utilize artificial sweeteners. We believe that natural sweeteners such as honey, molasses, maple syrup and coconut sugar are more easily assimilated by the body. Like anything else, moderation is key when using natural sweeteners!

You will notice that we will include coconut sugar into many of our recipes needing a sweetener. That is because it contains a fiber called inulin. Inulin may slow glucose absorption and therefore has a lower glycemic index than regular sugar (even though the caloric count is the same). Cinnamon actually begins to taste sweet to the palate after sugar is significantly reduced in the diet. We recommend any sweetener as an intermittent treat and not as a daily staple.

We are not advocates of Aspartame, Sucralose, Saccharin or Acesulfame K nor are we advocates of other common "natural" sweeteners such as high fructose corn syrup or agave nectar. These ultra processed sweeteners are believed to spike insulin levels. There is an abundant amount of published information on the subject and we encourage readers to decide for themselves.

MSG

Another additive that we avoid with great effort is monosodium glutamate, also known as MSG. MSG is a chemical flavor enhancer added to many processed foods. This food additive has been reported to affect individuals in a variety of ways including headaches, gastric upset and joint pain. The tricky thing about MSG is that it is added to many organically processed foods as well as mainstream processed foods. Selecting organic processed food is still selecting processed food!

With its many hidden names, you must research the names of MSG and read your labels. We help coach our clients through this maze and many are shocked at how much is in our food supply and how good they begin to feel after eliminating it from their diet. One easy way to avoid MSG is to simply eat real foods in their most natural states. By creating your own snacks, meals and desserts, you can live without these dangerous chemicals that often wreak havoc on the human body.

Clean 15 and Dirty Dozen

One of the biggest concerns among our clients is whether or not to purchase organically grown produce. It can be costly in comparison to conventionally grown produce. Each year in April, an organization called the Environmental Wellness Group (EWG) creates a list of produce tested from major produce growers and ranks them in order of pesticide residues. This is an interesting list to reference because the same items tend to remain in the top and bottom of the list each year. In 2016 strawberries topped the list as one of the most chemically laden items surpassing apples, which had been at the top of the list for 5 running years prior.

Since organically grown produce isn't always accessible or affordable to everyone, their guide can be a helpful resource to consumers. You can find the current EWG Shopper's Guide at www.ewg.org and determine which items you prefer to purchase based on the list. We highly recommend to our clients buying organic produce on the "Dirty Dozen" list whenever possible.

No Bake Simplicity

Turkey Taco Salad with Cranberry Salsa

Turkey Taco Salad

3 Tbs	extra virgin olive oil
12 oz	turkey breast, shredded
1	medium red bell pepper, sliced
1	medium yellow bell pepper, sliced
1/3 c	onion, chopped
3 cloves	garlic, minced
1/2 c	canned black beans
1 tsp	chili powder
1 tsp	ground cumin
1 tsp	cayenne
8 c	romaine lettuce, torn
1/4 c	fresh cilantro, chopped
1	avocado, cubed
8	cherry tomatoes, sliced
1/4 c	crushed tortilla chips (We used Trader Joe's Blue Corn Quinoa and Chia Seed Chips)

Combine olive oil, onion, garlic, chili powder, cumin and cayenne in a small skillet and lightly saute until flavors have infused. Set aside.

Combine lettuce, cilantro, peppers and tomatoes and black beans in a large bowl. Toss with olive oil mixture and coat evenly. Divide into individuals servings and top with turkey, tomatoes and avocado and chips. For the grand finale top with desired amount of cranberry salsa!

316 kcal Per Serving (makes 4) / Fat: 18g / Carbohydrate: 19.5g / Fiber: 6.5g / Protein: 19.25g

Cranberry Salsa

1 1/2 c	fresh or frozen cranberries
1/2	apple, cored and sliced (peeling optional)
1	jalapeno chili, chopped
4 Tbs	coconut sugar
2 Tbs	fresh cilantro, chopped
1/2	lime, squeezed
	dash of Himalayan pink salt

Combine all ingredients in a food processor and chop to desired consistency. Serve at room tempe56rature and refrigerate unused salsa right away.

78 kcal Per Serving (makes 4) / Fat: 0.15g / Carbohydrate: 19.3g / Fiber: 2.1g / Protein: 0.05g

- Turkey is a lean protein that is rich in the amino acid called L-Tryptophan that gives us better sleep. Cranberries are low in calories. 1/2 cup of cranberries contains just 25 calories! They keep the urinary tract healthy, improve immune function and help decrease blood pressure.

Kale and Pomegranate Salad with Vinaigrette

8 oz	kale, chopped
1/2	small red onion, thinly sliced
1/2 c	pomegranate seeds
1/4 c	slivered almonds
1/4 c	crumbled feta cheese
3 Tbs	champagne vinegar
2 Tbs	extra virgin olive oil
1 Tbs	dijon mustard
1 Tbs	honey
1/4 tsp	sea salt
1/4 tsp	coarse ground black pepper
	pinch cayenne pepper

Place kale, red onions, pomegranate seeds, almonds, and crumbled feta. In a separate bowl, whisk together champagne vinegar, olive oil, dijon mustard, honey, salt, and pepper (along with cayenne pepper if you desire). Once well combined, pour the dressing over the kale mixture and toss to coat. Before serving, refrigerate dressed salad 20 minutes before serving so that the flavors have time to develop. Garnish with a few extra pomegranate seeds.

121 kcal per serving (makes 6) / Fat: 8g / Carbohydrate: 10g / Fiber: 2g / Protein: 3g

Pear and Blue Cheese Salad

1 head	leaf lettuce, chopped
2 c	arugula
2	crisp pears, thinly sliced
3 oz	Roquefort cheese, crumbles (or another blue cheese)
1/4 c	hazelnuts, roasted and chopped
3	Tbs balsamic vinegar
3	Tbs extra virgin olive oil
1/4	tsp sea salt
	freshly ground black pepper

Add chopped leaf lettuce, arugula, and pear into a large bowl and toss. To the salad, add in first the balsamic vinegar and toss to coat; then add the olive oil and toss once more (it is important to add the oil after the vinegar to insure the balsamic vinegar will coat the lettuce). Just before plating, top with crumbled Roquefort, hazelnuts, salt and pepper. Toss lightly once more and serve.

187 kcal per serving (makes 6) / Fat: 13.5g / Carbohydrate: 11.3g / Fiber-2.5g / Protein: 5.3g

- Kale is an excellent anti-inflammatory and rich in iron. It has more calcium than milk which makes is an ideal source for vegetarians. Pomegranates consists of three times the amount of antioxidants as both red wine or green tea. It also has anti-tumor properties. This hearty salad is perfect for colder weather because both kale and pomegranates are in season during the colder months.
- The fiber-rich pear is good for the heart. Pear and Bleu cheese are a classic combination. This salad is great as a side dish but can easily become a main course by adding a grilled chicken breast or a filet of salmon.

Orange and Broccoli Slaw with Cranberries

12 oz	bag broccoli slaw mix
2 c	shredded cabbage
1/2 c	green onions, chopped
1	small garlic clove
1/2 c	dried cranberries
1/4 c	fat free Greek yogurt
3 Tbs	orange juice, fresh squeezed
2 Tbs	white wine vinegar
2 Tbs	balsamic vinegar
1 Tbs	coconut oil, melted
1 tsp	orange zest
1 tsp	honey
1/2 tsp	sea salt

In a food processor, combine Greek yogurt, garlic, orange juice, both vinegars, coconut oil, honey, and salt then blend until smooth. Combine broccoli slaw, cabbage, cranberries, and orange zest in a large bowl. Add the dressing and toss to combine.

95 kcal per serving (makes 6) / Fats: 2.3g / Carbohydrate: 18g / Fiber: 2.7g / Protein: 2.4g

• Broccoli is considered to be one of the world's healthiest foods. It is a cruciferous vegetable. Broccoli is known to be an excellent estrogen flusher in the body. Fat free Greek yogurt is a great substitute for mayonnaise-based recipes.

Strawberry Salad

Strawberry Salad

Lime Vinaigrette

1/4 c	extra virgin olive oil
1/4 c	lime juice
1/4 c	honey
1/4 c	balsamic vinegar
	salt and pepper

Salad

3 c	baby spinach
1 1/2 c	strawberries, sliced
1/2 c	feta, crumbled
1/3 c	toasted almonds, sliced
1/4 c	lime vinaigrette
	salt and pepper to taste

Whisk together all ingredients and set aside. In a large bowl combine spinach, strawberries and vinaigrette to taste and toss together. Mix in almonds, feta, salt and pepper. Refrigerate and store remaining vinaigrette for up to one week.

246 kcal per serving (makes 4) / Fat: 16.4g / Carbohydrate: 24.7g / Fiber: 1.6g / Protein: 2.8g

Strawberry Vinaigrette

1/2 lb	fresh strawberries, trimmed and sliced
2 Tbs	sherry vinegar
2 Tbs	olive oil
2 Tbs	honey
1/4 tsp	salt
1/4 tsp	freshly ground black pepper

Whisk together vinegar and honey in a small bowl. Add the sliced strawberries and stir to coat. Let sit for 30 minutes. Place all the ingredients in a blender and puree until smooth. Taste and adjust salt and pepper to taste if necessary. Serve immediately or store in an airtight container in refrigerator for up to a week.

74 kcal per serving (makes 6) / Fat: 4.8g / Carbohydrate: 9.2g / Fiber: ?g / Protein: 0.03g

- Strawberries are rich in Vitamin C. Due to the pesticide levels of conventionally grown strawberries according the the Environmental Wellness Group, we highly recommend buying organic strawberries whenever possible.

Thai-inspired slaw

3 c	green cabbage, shredded
2 c	napa cabbage, shredded
1 c	red cabbage, shredded
2	carrots, shredded
1	bell pepper, julienned
1	serrano chili, seeded and julienned
1/2 c	green onion, chopped
1/4 c	unsalted cashews, roasted
1/3 c	rice wine vinegar
1 Tbs	red pepper flakes (optional)
1 Tbs	fresh basil, chopped
2 tsp	fresh mint, chopped
2 tsp	fresh lime juice
2 tsp	honey
1 clove	garlic, minced
1 tsp	cilantro, chopped
1 tsp	fish sauce (optional)
1/2 tsp	fresh ginger, peeled and minced
1 Tbs	sesame oil

Combine vinegar, red pepper flakes, all the fresh herbs, honey, garlic, ginger, and lime juice in a medium bowl then slowly whisk in the sesame oil. In a larger bowl, toss together all three cabbages, bell pepper, chili, green onion, and cashews. Drizzle vinaigrette over the slaw and toss to combine. Chill 30 minutes before serving.

93 kcal per serving (makes 6) / Fat: 4.5g / Carbohydrate: 11g / Fiber: 3g / Protein: 2.3g

- Sesame oil is rich in omega-6 fatty acids. Its nutty flavor enhances traditional Asian dishes. The linoleic acid provides antibacterial and anti-inflammatory properties and are great for softening the skin.

Classic Wedge Salad

1 head	iceberg lettuce
2	small tomatoes, chopped
4 strips	cooked turkey bacon, cut into 1/2 inch pieces
1/2 c	plain fat free Greek yogurt
1/4 c	blue cheese, finely crumbled
1 Tbs	lemon, juiced
1 Tbs	white vinegar
1/2 tsp	coarse ground black pepper
1/2 tsp	honey
1/4 tsp	Worcestershire sauce
1/4 tsp	garlic powder
1/4 tsp	onion powder
	minced chives, for garnish

Remove the outer layer of the head of lettuce and quarter. In a medium bowl, combine Greek yogurt, blue cheese, lemon juice, vinegar, black pepper, Worcestershire sauce, honey, garlic powder, and onion powder; whisky together until all the ingredients are combined. To plate, arrange iceberg wedges on chilled plates and spoon the blue cheese dressing over top. Sprinkle chopped tomatoes, turkey bacon crumbles, and chives over top of the dressed lettuce. Serve chilled.

106 kcal Per Serving (makes 4) / Fat: 4g / Carbohydrate: 9.5g / Fiber: 2g / Protein: 7g

Creamy Parmesan Vinaigrette

2 Tbs	white wine vinegar
2 Tbs	plain fat free Greek yogurt
1 Tbs	grated parmesan cheese
1/8 tsp	salt
1/4 tsp	fresh ground black pepper

Whisk vinegar, Greek yogurt and olive oil together in a small bowl. Add grated parmesan cheese, salt, and pepper to taste.

68 kcal Per serving (makes 6) / Fat: 7.2g / Carbohydrate: 0.3g / Fiber: 0g / Protein: 1g

---

- Greek yogurt is rich in probiotics which helps the intestinal flora. Colon health is just as important as any other part of the body! The wedge salad is a classic steakhouse staple. This recipe replaces the traditional version which is typically loaded full of fat and excess calories and is full of flavor. Go ahead, give it a try!
- Parmesan cheese contains both calcium and Vitamin D. Vitamin D regulates Vitamin D absorption.

Cranberry Apple Slaw

1 bag	Trader Joe's Organic Broccoli Slaw
1/2 c	plain fat free Greek yogurt
1/3 c	dried cranberries
3 1/2 Tbs	red wine vinegar
3 Tbs	coconut sugar
1/4 c	sliced toasted almonds
1	small pple, diced
	Salt and pepper to taste

In a large bowl mix other ingredients until thoroughly combined, then fold in almonds and add salt and pepper to taste. Refrigerate for 1 hour before serving.

167 kcal Per Serving (makes 5) / Fat: 8.6g / Carbohydrate: 22.7g / Fiber: 2.7g / Protein: 1.7g

• This delicious slaw is broccoli based and rich in antioxidants with the cranberries.

Cranberry Apple Slaw

Peach Basil Salad

Salad

1 1/2 lbs	of tomatoes (any variety), roughly chopped
4	ripe peaches, sliced into wedges
1/2 c	crumbled feta cheese
1 Tbs	chia seeds
	small basil leaf garnish

Combine the tomatoes and peaches in a bowl and lightly drizzle with the dressing. Top with the feta cheese and chia seeds. Lightly garnish with fresh basil. Serve chilled.

Basil Vinaigrette

1/4 c	fresh basil leaves, torn
1/4 c	red onion, chopped
1/4 c	extra virgin olive oil
1/4 c	red wine vinegar
1 1/2 Tbs	honey
1 tsp	dijon mustard
	sea salt and ground white pepper

Combine the basil, onion, olive oil, vinegar, honey and mustard in a blender until the dressing emulsifies and the basil is pureed. Add a dash of salt and pepper to taste.

(Recipe for Marinated Teriyaki Pork Tenderloin, pictured, is on page 160)

194 kcal Per Serving (makes 6) / Fat: 12g / Carbohydrate: 20.4g / Fiber: 3.8g / Protein: 4g

• When most people think of preparing a salad they automatically think that it needs to consist of greens, but what we tell our clients is that a salad can be whatever you want as long as it includes fresh produce. That opens up endless options.

Peach Basil Salad

Cucumber and Mint Salad

4	small pickling cucumbers, thinly sliced
1 tsp	salt
1/4	small red onion, thinly sliced
1/4 c	sherry wine vinegar
2 Tbs	extra virgin olive oil
1 Tbs	honey
1/4 tsp	white pepper
1/4 c	fresh mint, chopped
1/8 tsp	ground coriander
	freshly ground black pepper to taste

Begin by combining cucumbers and salt in a bowl and let them sit for 30 minutes (this will remove excesses water from the cucumbers). After the cucumbers have rested, drain the excess water and add the red onion and fresh mint to the bowl. In a separate bowl, whisk together sherry wine vinegar, honey, white pepper, and ground coriander; then slowly drizzle in the olive oil. Add the vinaigrette to the salad and toss to combine. Garnish with a mint leaf and freshly ground black pepper.

65 kcal Per Serving (makes 6) / Fat: 4.7g / Carbohydrate: 6g / Fiber: 1.5g / Protein: 0.75g

• Cucumbers are an excellent way to stay hydrated and are low in calories. Mint is excellent in promoting healthy digestion. This salad is great paired with many types of fish but could also be an exceptional pairing with a grilled lamb chop.

Apple and Walnut Salad

2	apples, diced
2 ribs	celery, diced
2 Tbs	lemon juice
1/2 c	walnuts, chopped
1/3 c	dried cranberries
1/2 c	plain fat free Greek yogurt
1 Tbs	honey
1/2 tsp	lemon zest
1/8 tsp	white pepper
	salt and freshly ground black pepper to taste

Place apples, celery, and cranberries in a bowl and toss with the lemon juice. In a separate bowl combine Greek yogurt, honey, lemon zest, and white pepper then stir until evenly incorporated. Add the dressing with the apple mixture and season with salt and pepper to taste.

141 kcal Per Serving (makes 6) / Fat: 6g / Carbohydrate: 18g / Fiber: 3g / Protein: 3.25g

Watermelon Salad

1	seedless watermelon, cubed
1	small red onion, thinly sliced
1/2 c	fresh mint leaves, thinly sliced
3 oz	feta cheese, crumbles
2 Tbs	extra-virgin olive oil
1 Tbs	red wine vinegar
1 Tbs	lime juice
1	medium cucumber, diced
	coarse black pepper to taste

In a medium bowl, add the sliced onion, vinegar, and lime juice; let the onion slices marinate for 10 minutes. After 10 minutes, slowly whisk in the olive oil. In a separate bowl, add the cubed watermelon, cucumber, and feta then toss together. Pour the onion mixture over the watermelon then sprinkle the chopped mint and black pepper over top. Serve chilled.

200 kcal per serving (recipe makes 6) / Fat: 7.7g / Carbohydrate: 31.3g / Fiber: 2.2g / Protein: 5.2g

---

- Did you know that biting into apples are a great way to help whiten the teeth? Its also a great way to stimulate the necessary saliva in your mouth to aid in the digestion process! This apple salad is a great dish to have anytime of the year; try this wonderful autumn salad to accompany an assortment of main courses.

- Watermelons are mostly water and are loaded with nutrients, including potassium which is a water balance regulator. This salad is refreshing on any summer afternoon.

Zi Olive Knoxville

We appreciate our friends Eric and JC Muffett at Zi Olive Knoxville. They carry high quality flavor infused olive oils and delicious balsamic vinegars. Olive oil is rich in omega-3 fats and balsamic vinegar is a great digestive aid rich in antioxidants. After sampling a ton of winning combinations at their store, we asked them to create some special blends just for the readers of the *Taste of Totality* cookbook. Here is a small representation of the many delicious vinaigrettes and marinade recipes that can be created to add excitement to your homemade culinary creations. These can be used on salads, vegetables, pastas and meats to add flair and flavor. Visit their website: www. zioliveknox.com.

- Making more or less Vinaigrette: Stick to a rough ratio of 3 parts olive oil to 1 part balsamic vinegar and scale up or down according to taste. To add more flavor, use less olive oil or add more balsamic vinegar. Smaller amounts are easily whisked together in a small bowl and poured immediately over salad.

Zi Olive: Blood Orange and Fig Vinaigrette

3 Tbs	Zi Olive Blood Orange Olive Oil
1 Tbs	Zi Olive Fig Balsamic Vinegar
1 tsp	honey (optional)

Whisk together and enjoy on green salad or fruit salad. Great marinade for chicken or pork as well!

84 kcal Per Serving (makes 5) / Fat: 9g / Carbohydrate: 1.8g / Fiber: 0g / Protein: 0g

Zi Olive: Meyer Lemon and Key Lime Vinaigrette

3 Tbs	Zi Olive Meyer Lemon Olive Oil
1 Tbs	Zi Olive Key Lime Balsamic Vinegar
1 tsp	honey (optional)

Whisk together and enjoy on salad, fruit or brush on while grilling fish or chicken.

82 kcal Per Serving (makes 5) / Fat: 9g / Carbohydrate: 1.4g / Fiber: 0g / Protein: 0g

Zi Olive: Persian Lime and Garlic Cilantro Vinaigrette

3 Tbs	Zi Olive Persian Lime Olive Oil
1 Tbs	Zi Olive Garlic Cilantro Balsamic Vinegar
1 tsp	honey (optional)

Whisk together and enjoy on salad, avocados, great marinade for chicken too!

84 kcal Per Serving (makes 5) / Fat: 9g / Carbohydrate: 1.8g / Fiber: 0g / Protein: 0g

Zi Olive: Italian Herb Vinaigrette

3 Tbs	Zi Olive Italian Herb Olive Oil
1 Tbs	Zi Olive Traditional Balsamic Vinegar

Whisk together and enjoy on salad. Use for bread dipping or marinating too.

To emulsify, add one of the following:

1 tsp	dijon mustard per 1 Tbs Zi Olive Balsamic Vinegar
1/8 tsp	mustard powder
1 tsp	honey

Optional extras: minced garlic, minced shallots, minced fresh herbs, dried herbs. These vinaigrettes will keep on the counter for several weeks (refrigerate if you add any fresh ingredients). If the oil and vinegar separate, just whisk or shake well before serving.

84 kcal Per Serving (makes 5) / Fat: 9g / Carbohydrate: 1.8g / Fiber: 0g / Protein: 0g

Zi Olive: Hickory Smoked Olive Oil and Garlic Balsamic Marinade

2 Tbs	Zi Olive Hickory or Mesquite Smoked Olive Oil
3 Tbs	Zi Olive Garlic Balsamic Vinegar
1 tsp	honey (optional)
	salt and pepper

Whisk well then marinade beef, chicken, or pork for 3-4 hours. The balsamic vinegar will tenderize the meat and the olive oil makes it so moist!

Optional extras: garlic cloves, shallots, minced fresh herbs, dried herbs

70 kcal Per Serving (makes 5) / Fat: 7g / Carbohydrate: 2g / Fiber: 0g / Protein: 0g

Zi Olive: Jalapeno Olive Oil and Smoked Balsamic Marinade

2 Tbs	Zi Olive Jalapeno Olive Oil (or House Blend Olive Oil)
3 Tbs	Zi Olive Smoked Balsamic Vinegar
1 tsp	honey (optional)
	salt and pepper

Whisk well. Marinade chicken or pork for 3-4 hours. Marinade beef 6-8 hours. The balsamic vinegar will tenderize the meat and the olive oil makes it so moist!

Optional extras: garlic cloves, shallots, minced fresh herbs, dried herbs

70 kcal Per Serving (makes 5) / Fat: 7g / Carbohydrate: 2g / Fiber: 0g / Protein: 0g

Zi Olive: Pecan Smoked Olive Oil and Mango Balsamic Marinade

2 Tbs	Zi Olive Pecan Smoked Olive Oil
1 Tbs	Zi Olive Mango Balsamic
1 tsp	honey (optional)
	salt and pepper

Whisk well. Marinade chicken 3-4 hours or brush on fish while cooking.

59 kcal Per Serving (makes 5) / Fat: 6.2g / Carbohydrate: 1.4g / Fiber: 0g / Protein: 0g

Zi Olive: Mesquite Smoked Olive Oil and Kentucky Bourbon Balsamic Marinade

2 Tbs	Zi Olive Mesquite Smoked Olive Oil
1 Tbs	Zi Olive Kentucky Bourbon Balsamic Vinegar
1 tsp	honey (optional)
	salt and pepper

Whisk well. Great marinade for steak or burgers!

59 kcal Per Serving (makes 5) / Fat: 6.2g / Carbohydrate: 1.4g / Fiber: 0g / Protein: 0g

Italian Appetizer Kabobs

Italian Appetizer Kabobs

10	cherry tomatoes
10	small mozzarella balls
10	basil leaves
10	thin slices of prosciutto ham
10	toothpicks
3 Tbs	balsamic vinegar
	cracked pepper

On each toothpick assemble one tomato, cheese ball, basil leaf and ham slice. Complete making all ten. Top with vinegar and cracked pepper.

212 kcal per serving (makes 5) / Fat: 13.6g / Carbohydrate: 2.5g / Fiber: 0.5g / Protein: 20.3g

- When you need something quick, tasty and inexpensive, this little appetizer is your answer. Toothpicks, prosciutto, basil, cherry tomatoes and fresh mozzarella do the trick. We love basil for its sweet earthy aroma and its high Vitamin K content. Tomatoes are rich in coumaric acid and chlorogenic acid which actually repair damage caused by smoking!

Kombucha Poolside Spritzers

Basic Recipe for any Kombucha Spritzer:

10 oz	bottle flavored kombucha tea (We used GT's and Synergy Brands)
2 oz	can or bottle sparkling flavored water (We used LaCroix)
1/4 c	fresh cut fruit

Add ice to the glass, add Kombucha, sparkling water and fruit and stir. Mix and match any flavor, serve and enjoy!

Strawberry Splash:

10 oz	GT Strawberry Serenity Kombucha
2 oz	LaCroix Peach Pear Sparkling Water
1/4 c	strawberries and kiwi, chopped

86 kcal Per Serving (makes 1) / Fat: .15g / Carbohydrate: 20g / Fiber: 1.1g / Protein: .5g

Cranberry Delight

10 oz	GT Cosmic Cranberry Kombucha
2 oz	LaCroix Cran Raspberry Sparkling Water
1/4 c	blackberries and raspberries, chopped in half

58 kcal Per Serving (makes 1) / Fat: .18g / Carbohydrate: 13.5g / Fiber: 1.8g / Protein: 0.25g

Tropical Nectar

10 oz	GT Guava Goddess Kombucha
2 oz	LaCroix Mango Sparkling Water
1/4 c	fresh pineapple, chopped

80 kcal Per Serving / Fat: .05g / Carbohydrate: 20g / Fiber: 0.6g / Protein: 0.2g

- Kombucha has been around for years in Japan. It is a lightly, effervescent sweetened tea that is known for its benefits of containing probiotics. You can find high quality kombucha teas in the refrigerated section of health food stores and some major grocery store chains. These spritzers are not meant to be powerfully sweet, but a light and refreshing alternative to a basic flavored water. While you sip on these, you can also reap the benefit of fresh fruits too.

Kombucha Poolside Spritzers

Cupids Coconut Cream Smoothie

Cupid's Coconut Cream Smoothie

1 c	fresh strawberries
1/2	frozen banana
1/2 c	frozen cherries
1/2 c	almond milk
1/4 c	canned coconut cream (refrigerated overnight)
1 tsp	vanilla extract
1 Tbs	sweet cocoa nibs
1 Tbs	coconut chips

Begin by adding almond milk, coconut cream and vanilla into a blender. Add banana and cherries and strawberries last. Blend until all ingredients are blended without any chunks remaining. Pour into a glass and top with coconut chips and cocoa nibs. Add a small skewer of pierced strawberries for flair, serve and enjoy!

313 kcal Per Serving (makes 1) / Fat: 15.4g / Carbohydrate: 43g / Fiber: 6.8g / Protein: 4g

• This fun smoothie is dairy-free and vegan. Bananas are rich in potassium, which regulates water balance in the body. Cherries are rich in antioxidants, which is good for the heart and strawberries are added for a big dose of Vitamin C. Here you have a heart-healthy drink to serve to those you love.

Mango Coconut Chia Pudding

1 c	unsweetened almond milk
1/2 c	mango, diced
2 1/2 Tbs	chia seeds
2 Tbs	shredded coconut, unsweetened

Add all ingredients into a resealable container (such as a mason jar) and stir. Place lid on container and refrigerate overnight, or at least 6 hours. This time allows for the chia seeds to absorb the liquid and produce a pudding-like consistency. Serve chilled or store up to a week in the refrigerator.

150 kcal Per Serving (makes 2) / Fat: 1.03g / Carbohydrate 13.3g / Fiber: 7.9g / Protein: 4.9g

Peanut Butter and Chocolate Protein Bars

1 1/2 c	rolled oats
1/2 c	brown rice crisp cereal
3 scoops	protein powder
1 Tbs	chia seeds
1/3 c	honey
1/2 c	peanut butter
1-2 Tbs	water
1 tsp	vanilla extract
pinch	salt

Place oats in food processor and blend until oats are a flour consistency. Combine oat flour, rice cereal, protein powder, and chia seeds in medium bowl. In a small pan on medium heat, add honey along with peanut butter, vanilla, salt, and water. Heat until warm and easy to stir. Pour peanut butter mixture over oats and stir well. Take mixture and press into in a 9" x 5" greased loaf pan. Place loaf pan in refrigerator for 20-30 before slicing. Store in an airtight container for up to a week in the refrigerator.

160 kcal Per Serving (makes 12) / Fat: 6g / Carbohydrate: 17g / Fiber: 1.7g / Protein: 10g

- Mango and chia partner together in this dynamic tropical pudding to give you flavor, energy, rich antioxidants, fiber, and Omega-3 fatty acids.

- The word chia means energy and the Mayan Indians have used chia seeds for years as an energy source. They are a healthy source of omega-3 fats too!

Oven Creations

Scott's Hawaiian Baguette

12"	whole grain baguette
4 Tbs	garlic, crushed
8 slices	provolone cheese
8 slices	prosciutto
1	avocado, sliced
1	mango
	sea salt in grinder

Preheat oven to 375 F. Cut baguette in half crosswise and lengthwise. Spread crushed garlic each of the pieces of baguette. Toast in the oven until slightly crisp, about 5 min. Remove from the oven and add 2 slices of provolone and Prosciutto to each piece of baguette. Toast in the oven for an additional 3 min. Wash and slice avocado and mango. Remove baguette from the oven. Place avocado slices on top of the prosciutto. Grind salt over each piece of baguette before placing slices of mango on top.

230 kcal Per Serving (makes 4) / Fat: 9g / Carbohydrate: 26.5g / Fiber: 2.8g / Protein: 10.5g

• This light seasonal appetizer is sure to be a hit. It contains all of our favorites, including avocado. We love avocado for the rich brain and skin enhancing omega-3 fats.

Scott's Hawaiian Baguette

Roasted Red Pepper Hummus

1 1/2 c	cooked chickpeas, rinsed and drained (about 1 can)
2	red bell pepper
2 Tbs	almond butter
1 1/2 Tbs	extra-virgin olive oil
1 Tbs	water
1	garlic clove, minced
1	lemon, juiced
1/4 tsp	salt
1/4 tsp	smoked paprika
1/8 tsp	cayenne
pinch	cumin (optional)

Begin by setting oven to broil. Place red peppers on a sheet pan and roast in the oven for 10-15 minutes, turning every 5 minutes to ensure they roast evenly. Once roasted, allow the peppers to before removing the stem, seeds, and skin. In a high-powered blender, add the roasted peppers, chickpeas, garlic, lemon juice, almond butter, water, olive oil, salt, and all the spices. Blend until a smooth paste is formed (a few more teaspoons of water may be required), and taste for any additional salt. Serve alongside chopped carrots, celery, radishes, and any other raw vegetables. Store refrigerated in an airtight container for up to a week.

96 kcal Per Serving (makes 8) / Fat: 5.5g / Carbohydrate: 10.5g / Fiber: 1.6g / Protein: 3.5g

- Chickpeas are rich in protein and fiber. Try these recipes to add beneficial nutrients to your meals! This recipe takes traditional hummus and replaces tahini with almond butter and adds roasted red peppers to create a more flavorful spread. Enjoy with raw vegetables or spread on a grilled chicken breast.

Southwest Roasted Chickpeas

2 cans	chickpeas, drained
2 Tbs	extra virgin olive oil
1 Tbs	chili powder
1 tsp	smoked paprika
1/4 tsp	cayenne pepper
1/4 tsp	sea salt
1/4 tsp	garlic powder
1/2	lime, sliced into wedges

Preheat oven to 400 degrees. In a large bowl, combine chickpeas, olive oil, salt and all spices; mix to incorporate. Place chickpeas on a sheet pan lined with parchment paper. Bake the chickpeas for 25-30 minutes, or until they are crunchy on the outside and slightly soft in the middle. Serve warm or room temperature with the lime wedges.

158 kcal Per Serving (makes 5) / Fat: 7.5g / Carbohydrate: 18g / Fiber: 6g / Protein: 6g

- These roasted chickpeas are a good finger food when you want something crunchy to snack on, and the cayenne pepper provide an extra depth of flavor.

Vol Chicken Burger

2 lbs	ground chicken
1/2 c	finely chopped red onion
1/4 c	minced fresh cilantro
1 Tbs	freshly squeezed lime juice
1/4 c	orange juice
2 Tbs	barbeque sauce
	salt and pepper

Mix all ingredients together by hand in large bowl. Form patties and cook in the oven or on open flame at 400 degrees for 4 minutes per side (or until thoroughly cooked). Place on bun and garnish with orange wedges and chips of your choice.

179 kcal Per Serving (makes 6) / Fat: 2g / Carbohydrate: 5g / Fiber: 0.2g / Protein: 34.9g

- When football season comes around, tailgating food can include healthy food! Ground chicken is a lean protein. Marinated with fresh cilantro and orange juice kick these burgers up with antioxidants!

Vol Chicken Burger

Pumpkin Quinoa Snack bars

1 c	rolled oats
1 c	quinoa, rinsed
3/4 c	pure pumpkin puree
3 Tbs	natural peanut butter
3 Tbs	honey
1 Tbs	coconut oil, melted
1/2 tsp	cinnamon
1/8 tsp	nutmeg
1/2 tsp	baking powder
1/4 tsp	salt

Preheat oven to 350 degrees and grease a 9x9 inch baking dish with coconut oil. In a large bowl combine rolled oats, quinoa, baking powder, cinnamon, nutmeg, and salt; mix the dry ingredients to combine. Then add pumpkin puree, peanut butter, coconut oil, and honey. Stir until well incorporated. Add the batter to the greased 9x9, and spread it out evenly. Bake for 25- 30 minutes, or until the center is cooked through. Once baked, let the dish sit for 20 minutes before slicing into 12 pieces. Store refrigerated in an airtight container.

133 kcal Per Serving (makes 12) / Fat: 4.6 g / Carbohydrate: 20.3 g / Fiber: 2.3g / Protein: 4 g

- These longstanding foods make a great combo of antioxidants and a protein source when you need something on-the-go! The combination of oats, quinoa and peanut butter are sure to provide plenty of energy.

Banana oatmeal muffins

2 1/2 c	old fashioned rolled oats
1 c	fat free Greek yogurt
2	ripe bananas
1/2 c	honey
2 tsp	baking powder
1 tsp	baking soda
1 tsp	cinnamon
1 tsp	vanilla
1/8 tsp	salt

Preheat oven to 350 F. Place rolled oats in a food processor and blend for 20 seconds. After the oats have been blended, add the remaining ingredients to the food processor and process until a smooth batter is produced. Divide the batter into a muffin pan and bake for 18-20 minutes, or until slightly golden brown. Store in an airtight container for up to 1 week.

132 kcal Per serving (makes 12) / Fat: 1.3g / Carbohydrate: 28g / Fiber: 2.3g / Protein: 4g

- Homemade muffins are a great quick and easy way to have a portable snack without the processed junk so prevalent in today's packaged food supply. A rich source of potassium and fiber make these muffins worth making! Feel free to add walnuts, blueberries or shredded coconut to the batter to change up the flavor combination.

Totality Matcha Tea Bread Pudding

1 loaf	French bread, cut into 1-inch cubes
4 c	almond milk
2 tsp	matcha green tea powder
3	eggs, lightly beaten
2 c	coconut sugar
2 Tbs	vanilla extract
1 c	raisins
1 c	apple juice
1/4 tsp	pumpkin pie spice
3 Tbs	coconut oil, melted

Preheat oven to 350 F. Soak raisins for 15 minutes in freshly boiled hot apple juice removed from burner. Mix matcha powder in warmed almond milk with a small whisk until dissolved. Soak the bread in Matcha milk mix in a large mixing bowl. Break down and crush with hands until well mixed and all the milk mixture is absorbed. In a separate bowl, beat eggs, coconut sugar, vanilla extract, and pumpkin pie spice together. Gently stir into the bread mixture. Carefully stir the raisins (with juice drained) into the mixture. Pour coconut oil into the bottom of a 9" x 13" inch baking pan. Coat the bottom and the sides of the pan well with the oil. Pour in the bread mix and bake at 350 F for 35-45 minutes, until set. The pudding is done when the edges start getting a bit brown and pull away from the edge of the pan. Dish out into a small bowl and top with a small scoop of coconut or vanilla gelato and top with a small sprinkle of matcha powder. Serve and enjoy!

320 kcal Per Serving (makes 12) / Fat: 6g / Carbohydrate: 62.4g / Fiber: 1.7g / Protein: 6.2g

- Totality Green Tea Bread Pudding adds a touch of festive green for the holiday season, packs a punch of flavor and benefits your health. The key ingredient is powdered Matcha Green Tea. Matcha is combined with almond milk, then infused into the bread. Matcha is rich in antioxidants, specifically EGCg, which is recognized for cancer fighting properties by some. It's high in chlorophyll, which helps the immune system, increases metabolism and improves mental focus.

Fall Medley Granola

3 c	rolled oats
1/4 c	uncooked quinoa
1/2 c	honey
1/3 c	pumpkin puree
2 Tbs	coconut oil
1/2 c	raw almonds
1/2 c	raw pecans
1/2 c	raw pistachios
1/2 c	dried cranberries
2 tsp	cinnamon
1/4 tsp	nutmeg
1/4 tsp	allspice
1/2 tsp	salt
1/2 tsp	vanilla extract

Preheat oven to 325 F. In a small pan over medium heat, combine coconut oil and honey. Heat until the coconut oil is melted then set aside. In a large bowl, combine oats, quinoa, almonds, pecans, pistachios, cranberries, salt, and spices. Stir to combine and then add the honey mixture, pumpkin puree, and vanilla. Stir until the oats and nuts are coated. Transfer the mixture baking sheet that has been sprayed with cooking spray. Spread the granola mixture evenly on the baking sheet and bake for 20 minutes. Remove from the oven and give the mixture a stir. Return the granola to the oven and bake for an addition 10-15 minutes, or until the mixture is golden. Remove from the oven and let the granola cool to room temperature. Store in an airtight container for up to two weeks.

200 kcal per serving (makes 15) / Fat: 9.7g / Carbohydrate: 27.2g / Fiber: 3.4g / Protein: 4.5g

- This recipe allows anyone to enjoy the taste of fall anytime. Not only that, these powerhouse ingredients boost the immune system and contribute to a healthy body.

Michelle's Patchwork Pizza

Michelle's Patchwork Pizza

1 P28	High Protein Wrap (Found at Eddie's Health Shoppe in Knoxville)
bases	olive oil, BBQ sauce, marinara, pizza sauce, pesto, etc
topping	cooked chicken, crumbled ground beef, pepperoni, Canadian bacon, mushrooms, chopped spinach, fresh basil, sundried tomatoes, olives, artichoke hearts, olives, etc.

Divide the sections according to your desire and start applying base sauces in individual areas. Next layer chopped spinach over entire pizza crust. Then get creative. Let each family member "decorate" their section with desired toppings.

Bake in oven at 400 F until cheeses are fused together and toppings are thoroughly cooked. Let cool and cut according to individualized sections and enjoy.

Macros will vary depending on toppings. This example has marinara sauce, pepperoni, and mozzarella cheese.

240 kcal Per Serving (makes 4) / Fat: 14g / Carbohydrate: 11.75g / Fiber: 2g / Protein: 18.5g

How do you appease each family member when each one wants something different for dinner? We have the answer and it comes in the form of pizza! Patchwork pizza to be exact. We created this in our own household a year ago and it has been a requested hit ever since. We begin by using P28 High Protein Wraps. These are ideal to get a high protein source into the meal without having to use meat. It's perfect for vegetarians and a nice carb exception (or cheat) for people who generally stay away from a carb based diet. You can confidently eat this since the protein count is higher. One wrap contains 28 grams of protein! . Each family member can put their own base such as marinara, pizza sauce, olive oil or barbeque sauce and build their section from there. You can get as creative as you want.

- Experiment with a variety of bases: olive oil, marinara and BBQ sauce and layer the entire pizza with chopped spinach. This is a great way to sneak in a high source of iron without changing the flavor of the pizza.

Irish Meatball and Oven-Roasted Potatoes

Totality Irish Meatball

2 lbs	ground turkey (bison or ground beef can substituted)
1/2	purple onion
2	large carrots
1	red bell pepper (stem removed)
1	medium zucchini
1/4 c	cabbage
2	crushed garlic cloves
1/4 c	select fresh green herb (parsley or cilantro)
1	egg white
1 tsp	dried thyme
2 tsp	balsamic vinegar
1/2 c	panko bread crumbs
	salt and pepper to taste
	olive oil

Put ground meat into mixing bowl and set aside. Combine all vegetables, garlic and herbs into a food processor and blend until liquefied. Pour liquid mixture into meat and work in. Add egg white, thyme, vinegar, and desired amounts of salt and pepper. Blend well with hands. Form 5-6 equal sized meatballs onto an olive oil coated broiler pan. Bake at 400 F for 30 minutes or until done. Different meats need varied cooking times.

Oven-Roasted Potatoes

1 lb	extra small yellow potatoes
	salt and pepper
2 tsp	powdered garlic
1 tsp	dried oregano
	olive oil

Preheat oven to 350 F. Wash potatoes and put into a large bowl. Drizzle with olive oil and toss until oil is coated evenly. Lay them out onto a baking sheet and sprinkle with salt, pepper and spices. Cook for approximately 40 minutes or until tender. Remove and plate.

354 kcal Per Serving (makes 6) / Fat: 11.6g / Carbohydrate: 26.5g / Fiber: 2.5g / Protein: 32g

* The Irish generally cook with pork, beef or lamb. We've added our own Totality twist to this dish by creating the meatball with ground turkey for a lighter option. You can sneak veggies into this meatball by pureeing them in a food processor and making that the main staple of your marinade. These large meatballs may look only like meat, but they are so much more!

Irish Meatball and Oven-Roasted Potatoes

Zesty Zucchini Pizza with Lamb and Turkey

Crust

4 c	zucchini, shredded
1 tsp	salt
1/2 c	fresh grated parmesan and mozzarella cheese (mixed)
1/3 c	almond flour
2 cloves	garlic, minced
2 1/2 tsp	Italian seasonings
1	large egg, beaten
1/4 tsp	salt

Preheat oven to 550 F. Place shredded zucchini into a large bowl with one 1 tsp of salt and mix well. Let sit for 20 minutes. Put zucchini into a piece of cheesecloth (using your clean hands) and squeeze the excess moisture out of the zucchini; discard the water. Place the zucchini back into the bowl, (using your hands), mix in the cheese, almond flour, garlic, Italian seasonings, egg, and the remaining 1/4 tsp salt. Pat it down thoroughly until tightly formed together.

Use a parchment-lined baking sheet. Place the zucchini crust mixture onto the parchment paper. Using your hands spread the mixture to form a circle about 12 inches in diameter, keeping the crust about 1/2-inch thick. Pinch the edges up so that it forms a nice edge. Pre-bake the Zucchini Pizza Crust for approximately 8 minutes or until the crust begins to brown at the edges. Remove from the oven and transfer onto a solid surface.

Toppings

1/2 lb	ground lamb
1/2 lb	ground turkey
1 Tbs	garlic, minced
1/2 c	marinara sauce
1/4 c	kalamata olives
1/2 c	sliced baby portabellas
1/4 c	sundried tomatoes
1/3 c	slivered almonds
	dried Italian seasonings to taste
	salt and pepper to taste
1 c	mozzarella
1/2 c	parmesan

Saute ground lamb and ground turkey together with minced garlic, salt and pepper. Set aside. You may use any commercial marinara sauce if you like. Then top with meat mixture, olives, portabella mushrooms, tomatoes, almonds, seasonings, and cheese. Once you have created your toppings, transfer the pizza back to the oven and bake for an additional 4 to 5 minutes or until the cheese is melted and pizza looks heated through. Remove pizza from oven and transfer to a solid surface. Let rest for 3 minutes before cutting into serving sizes.

668 kcal per serving (makes 3) / Fat: 44g / Carbohydrate: 21g / Fiber: 5.6g / Protein: 48.4g

- The greatest thing about this pizza is that it fits a wide variety of dietary needs including: Gluten-free, Paleo, Low Carb, Low Fat and can feed anyone hungry. If you or anyone in your family are reluctant to try veggies, this is a great way to incorporate them. The crust is made with grated zucchini, a beaten egg and almond flour. Zucchini is high in potassium and vitamin c and very low in calories. Potassium lessens the harmful effects of salt on the body. Lamb is commonly used in Mediterranean diets. It is an excellent source of all the B Vitamins, which helps with stress. Top this pizza with anything you have in your pantry or fridge and have fun with it!

Zesty Zucchini Pizza with Lamb and Turkey

Tennessee Tailgating Nachos

Tennessee Tailgating Nachos

1 lb	lean ground turkey
12 oz	barbecue sauce (add more or less to taste)
1	large lime, juiced
	salt and pepper
1	large apple, chopped
1/2 c	Kalamata olives sliced
4-5	banana peppers from a jar, sliced
1 lb	bag corn chips (approximately 50 chips)
2 c	colby jack cheese, shredded
1/2 c	nonfat plain Greek yogurt
1 Tbs	hot sauce (any variety)
2	medium tomatoes, chopped

Saute ground turkey with salt and pepper to taste and fresh lime juice. Once that is almost done, add barbecue sauce, chopped apples and olives and mix together in the skillet until warmed. Set aside. Set out corn chips on a large baking sheet and top with barbeque turkey mixture, chopped banana peppers and colby jack cheese. Heat in oven on broil until cheese is melted. Remove and top with scattered dollops of Greek yogurt mixed with hot sauce, and evenly top with chopped tomatoes and serve. Happy tailgating!

465 kcal per serving (makes 5) / Fat: 18.9g / Carbohydrate: 37.2g / Fiber: 2.5g / Protein: 34.2g

- These aren't your average nachos; these are amped up nachos loaded with both flavor and nutrients. They are basically a meal to keep you full and on your toes for all of that football excitement. Ground turkey is very low in fat and high in protein and a great alternative to those wanting to eat a more health conscious diet. The apples and olives not only give an extra flare of flavor but provide a healthy source of vitamins, fiber and good fats that can sustain energy for those long tailgating days.

Peach cake

4 c	fresh peaches, chopped
1/2 c	coconut sugar (divided)
2 tsp	lemon juice
2 Tbs	coconut oil
2 tsp	vanilla extract
1/2 tsp	almond extract
2 large	eggs, beaten
2 c	organic all-purpose flour
1 tsp	baking powder
2 tsp	lemon rind, grated
1 tsp	cinnamon
1/2 tsp	nutmeg
2/3 c	milk
1/4 c	sliced toasted almonds

Preheat oven to 375 F. Combine peaches, 1/4 c sugar and lemon juice. Set aside. Beat 1/4 c sugar and oil at medium speed until blended. Add vanilla, almond extract and eggs and beat well. Combine flour, baking powder, lemon rind and spices. Add flour mixture to butter mixture alternating with milk, beginning and ending with flour mix. Spoon into an 8" springform pan coated with cooking spray. Spoon peaches over batter. Sprinkle with almonds and bake for 40 minutes or until golden.

256 kcal Per Serving (makes 10) / Fat: 6g / Carbohydrate: 46.3g / Fiber: 2g / Protein: 6g

- When you feel like splurging, this is a wonderful dessert to try when fresh peaches are in season. When you feel like going all out, this delicious alternative to peach pie is fantastic when served with vanilla ice cream.

Italian Cream cake

Cake

2 c	coconut sugar
1/2 c	butter
2	large egg yolks
2 c	organic all-purpose flour
1 tsp	baking soda
1 c	low-fat buttermilk
3/4 c	walnuts, chopped
2 tsp	vanilla extract
1 tsp	coconut extract
6	large egg whites at room temperature

Preheat oven to 350 F. Combine sugar and butter and beat at medium speed until blended. Add egg yolks one at a time. Beat well after each. Set aside. Combine flour, baking soda and stir well. Add to creamed mixture alternating with buttermilk, beginning and ending with flour mixture.

Stir in walnuts and extracts. Set aside. Beat egg whites at high speed with mixer until stiff. Fold egg whites into batter. Coat 3 nine-inch round cake pans with cooking spray only on bottoms, not sides. Line bottom of pans with wax paper. Coat wax paper with cooking spray and dust with flour. Pour batter into pan. Bake for 23 minutes. Cool in pans for 5 minutes. Turn out onto wire racks. Take off wax paper. Let cool.

Icing

3 Tbs	butter
2 1/2 pkgs	block-style cream cheese
2 c	powdered sugar
2 tsp	vanilla
1/2 c	large coconut flakes

Beat butter and cream cheese at high speed until fluffy. Gradually add in sugar and vanilla. Beat at low speed just until blended. Cover and chill.

Place one layer on plate and cover with 1 c of icing. Add the next layer and add 2/3 c icing. Add top layer. Spread with remaining icing and sprinkle with coconut flakes.

503 kcal Per Serving (makes 14) Fat: 26.5g Carbohydrate: 61.8g Fiber: 1.2g Protein: 8.2g

- This is one of Scott's favorites because it is a light cake that packs a lot of flavor. We have made this for family birthdays and it's always been the ultimate gift. This is a must-have for a no-guilt cheat meal!

Jicama Mango Slaw

2	mangos, peeled
1	carrot
1	red pepper
1/2	large jicama, peeled
1/2	jalapeno, seeded
1 Tbs	red wine vinegar
1 Tbs	lime juice
1 Tbs	honey
1 tsp	fresh mint, minced
1 tsp	fresh parsley

Julienne the fruit and vegetables and place in a large bowl. Whisk together the remaining ingredients and pour over the julienned veggies. Toast all ingredients together and chill for a minimum of 30 minutes before serving.

74 kcal per serving (makes 5) / Fat: 0g / Carbohydrate: 17.5g / Fiber: 2g / Protein: 1.2g

- Jicama is a root vegetable rich in Vitamin C, fiber and folate. It is an excellent soluble fiber that can boost digestive health. Mango is a Totality favorite. Research on this fruit has been found to protect against multiple cancers and improves digestion.

Chocolate oatmeal drops

1/3 c	brown sugar
1/4 c	coconut sugar
1/4 c	coconut oil, melted
2 tsp	vanilla
2 tsp	coconut extract
2	large egg whites
1 1/2 c	quick cooking oats
2/4 c	organic all-purpose flour
1/2 tsp	baking powder
1/3 c	semisweet chocolate chips

Preheat oven to 375 F. Combine sugars, oil, vanilla, coconut extract and egg whites. Beat on high speed until mixture is blended. Set aside. Combine oats, flour, baking powder, stir well and add to sugar mixture, stirring until moist. Stir in chocolate chips. Drop dough by tablespoon onto baking sheet coated with cooking spray. Bake for approximately 10 minutes. Remove from pan and cook on wire rack.

157 kcal Per Serving (makes 12) / Fat: 6.8g / Carbohydrate: 23.3g / Fiber: 1.4g / Protein: 2.5g

- For everyone who needs a little sweet treat in their life, this is a perfect example of enjoying decadence in moderation with pure satisfaction.

Stove Top Wonders

Spring Chili *It's all green and white!*

24 oz	chicken broth
4	15 oz cans of white beans -any variety (double if omitting chicken)
3	baked chicken breasts, chopped
1/2	white onion, chopped
3 cloves	garlic, chopped (or more to taste)
1 1/2 c	fresh cilantro, chopped
2	4 oz cans green chilies
1	small lime, juiced
1 c	grated Monterey Jack cheese (divided for portions)
1 Tbs	plain Greek yogurt per serving
4 Tbs	ground cumin
	salt and pepper

Sprinkle salt and pepper over chicken and bake at 350 degrees for 30 minutes. Remove from oven and chop.

Combine broth, beans, onion, garlic, cilantro, green chilies, lime juice, cumin, salt and pepper and simmer in crockpot or dutch oven over medium heat for 1 hour. Stir occasionally. Add chicken, stir and check for flavor balance. Adjust spices to taste and continue to simmer on low for another 45 minutes-1 hour.

Divide into bowls and top with grated cheese and Greek yogurt. A splash of green chili hot sauce is optional!

430 kcal Per Serving (makes 6) / Fat: 9.5g / Carbohydrate: 44.5g / Fiber: 12.5g / Protein: 46.4g

* This is the ideal dish for the early days of spring. Every ingredient in this dish is either green or white. It's a lighter take on red chili and is loaded with healthy dietary fiber, protein and antioxidants. This dish can be made with meat or made solely as a vegetarian dish. The white ingredients include chicken broth, an assortment of white beans, baked chicken breast, chopped garlic, onion, grated white monterrey jack cheese and a dollop of plain Greek yogurt in place of sour cream. The green ingredients you'll find are fresh cilantro, green chilies, and freshly squeezed lime juice. An assortment of salt, pepper and cumin help to enhance this dish and meld these flavors together beautifully.

Spring Chili

105

Summary Steak Salad

Steak

1	sirloin steak
1	lime, juiced
1 Tbs	olive oil
	salt and pepper

Vinaigrette

1	avocado
1 clove	garlic
1	lime, juiced
1/2 c	white balsamic vinegar
1/4 c	water
3 Tbs	olive oil
1/4 tsp	salt
1/4 tsp	pepper

Salad

1 heart	romaine lettuce
1	small cucumber, chopped
1/2	yellow bell pepper, sliced
1/2	orange bell pepper, sliced
1/4 c	blueberries
1/4	red onion, sliced
3 Tbs	roasted cashews, chopped

Begin by combining the steak with lime juice, salt, and pepper. Marinate for 30 minutes. Combine ingredients for the vinaigrette in a blender and blend until smooth. Set aside.

In a skillet over medium heat, add the olive oil then the marinaded steak. Cool 4-6 minutes per side on medium, or longer until desired doneness. Once done, let the steak rest for 10 minutes before slicing.

Arrange the remaining salad ingredients in a bowl, add steak atop the salad then drizzle with avocado vinaigrette. Serve with a few lime wedges and enjoy! Extra vinaigrette can be stored up to a week refrigerated in an airtight container.

304 kcal Per Serving (makes 2) / Fat: 13.5g / Carbohydrate: 19g / Fiber: 5g / Protein: 29.3g

* By including berries and several types of delicious vegetables, this salad takes full advantage of all that the summer growing season has to offer. The combination of lean sirloin steak and a vinaigrette made with avocado provide ample protein along with healthy fats that will keep you full.

Heart-Healthy Hominy Stew

4 tsp	cumin, divided
2 c	red onion, chopped
2 tsp	coconut sugar
4 Tbs	all purpose flour
2 Tbs	chili powder
3 cloves	garlic, minced
8 c	butternut squash (approx. 4 lbs), peeled and cubed
4 c	water
2	15 oz cans yellow hominy, drained
28 oz	chicken broth
1 c	red pepper, chopped

Heat stockpot at medium heat. Add 2 tsp cumin, onion and sugar. Saute until onion is browned. Stir in flour, chili powder and garlic, then saute for another minute. Add squash, water, hominy and broth. Bring to a boil. Cover. Reduce heat. Then simmer for 20 minutes. Uncover and simmer again until squash is very tender and stew thickens. Finally, stir in remaining cumin and red bell pepper. Cook for 5 more minutes until pepper softens. Then serve and enjoy this mega dose of tasty health!

174 kcal Per Serving (makes 6) / Fat: 0.01g / Carbohydrate: 38.8g / Fiber: 4.8g / Protein: 4.8g

• This delicious stew is both economical and healthy! Hominy is a grainy breakfast food made from maize kernels. It is thought to decrease the risk of diabetes and heart disease. Butternut squash is a power food. It is rich in phytonutrients and antioxidants. It is low in fat and high in fiber which means it is heart healthy. Cumin is a great source of iron, energy production and increases metabolism.

Turkey Scramble

2 lbs	lean ground turkey
1/2 c	diced red onion
3 cloves	garlic, minced
1 Tbs	cinnamon
1 Tbs	cumin
2 tsp	chili powder
1 tsp	cayenne pepper
	salt and pepper to taste
1/2 c	raisins
2	medium apples, diced
1 Tbs	coconut oil

In large skillet, melt coconut oil and add onions and garlic. Infuse oil and add turkey and spices. Saute' until turkey turns white and add raisins and apples to warm in mixture. Serve hot.

229 kcal Per Serving (makes 5) / Fat: 3.9g / Carbohydrate: 22.4g / Fiber: 2.1g / Protein: 28.9g

- We first showed this recipe with a client on Knoxville ABC affiliate, WATE -TV, as part of a segment on healthy cooking in his health journey. It is lean, tasty and can be varied according to items you have on hand. This dish is one of our main meal prep staples.

Rainbow Vegetable Medley

You can choose any of your favorite vegetables. Just make sure to create the rainbow!

1 1/2 Tbs	coconut oil
4 bulbs	garlic, chopped
1	medium red onion, sliced
2	zucchini squash, chopped
1	sweet red pepper, sliced
1	sweet yellow pepper, sliced
2 heads	chopped broccoli
8 oz	sliced mushrooms
1 Tbs	dried basil
1 Tbs	dried oregano
1 Tbs	dried thyme
1 Tbs	dried rosemary
dash	salt and pepper

Add oil to large saute' pan. Add garlic and onions and infuse oil. Add vegetables and saute' until tender.

104 kcal Per Serving (makes 5) / Fat: 4.8g / Carbohydrate: 13.5g / Fiber: 4.5g / Protein: 5.2g

- Anytime you add the colors of the rainbow from produce you are getting the widest variety of nutrients that nature has to offer. You are the artist in this dish. Which colors will be a part of your vibrant color pallet?

Christmas Confetti Pasta

Christmas Confetti Pasta

1 pkg	red lentil pasta
1	zucchini, julienned - 3"
1	yellow pepper, cut into strips
3/4 c	baby carrots, sliced
1/4 c	Kalamata olives
1/3 c	raisins
1	large apple, chopped
3 cloves	garlic, chopped
1 1/2 tsp	cumin
1 tsp	cinnamon
1/2 tsp	nutmeg
1/2 tsp	chili powder
	salt to taste
1 Tbs	coconut oil
2 Tbs	extra virgin olive oil
2 Tbs	grated parmesan cheese (optional)

Cook lentil pasta according to directions on package and set aside. Combine zucchini, orange pepper, baby carrots, olives, raisins, garlic and apple in large skillet with the coconut oil and spices and saute until mixture is slightly tender. Add red lentil pasta and mix together over low heat with olive oil for 1 minute until everything is mixed and flavors are infused. Top with cheese if desired. Serve warm.

Relax, enjoy and celebrate the holidays!

300 kcal Per Serving (makes 6) / Fat: 6.7g / Carbohydrates: 48.6g / Fiber: 4.5g / Protein: 12.7g

- This pasta is unique in that it is made from red lentils. It's a great dish for anyone looking for substantial protein and fiber. The pasta is dense, and unlike many of the other gluten-free pastas, doesn't get mushy when it's boiled. This dish is gluten-free, vegan and loaded with rich vitamins. The "confetti" is represented by the variety of multi-colored vegetables. We encourage you to play around with other bean pastas and vegetables to create your own version of this healthy dish!

Chicken Poblano Popper

1 lb	lean ground chicken
2	poblano peppers, seeded and diced
3 Tbs	cilantro, chopped
1	green onion, chopped
1 clove	garlic, minced
1 tsp	salt
1/2 tsp	pepper
1 Tbs	olive oil

In a large bowl, combine chicken, peppers, cilantro, green onion, garlic, salt, and pepper. Stir the mixture together and heat a skillet over medium heat. Add the olive oil to the pan and add the chicken mixture 1 heaping Tbs at a time to the pan. Cook each popper 8-10 minutes, flipping every 4 minutes to ensure even cooking. Serve warm or store in the refrigerator for up to 1 week.

53 kcal Per Popper (makes 12) / Fat: 1.7g / Carbohydrate: 0.7g / Fiber- 0.3g / Protein: 8.75g

Sweet Potato Salad

2 lbs	sweet potatoes, peeled and cut into cubes
1/2	sweet white onion, chopped
1	bell pepper, chopped (preferably red or yellow)
4	green onions, chopped
1/3 c	plain fat free Greek yogurt
1 Tbs	honey
1 tsp	smoked paprika
1/2 tsp	cumin
1/4 tsp	cayenne pepper
1/4 tsp	chili powder
1/4 tsp	salt

Bring a large pot of salted water to a boil over medium heat and add the diced sweet potatoes; cool for 15- 20 minutes (or until fully cooked but not mushy). Once cooked, drain the sweet potatoes and let cool in a colander. Add the cooked and cooled sweet potatoes to a large bowl along with the bell pepper, sweet onion, and green onions. In a separate bowl, combine Greek yogurt, honey, and all the spices. Whisk to combine, pour over the sweet potatoes mixture, and mix thoroughly. Add salt and fresh black pepper to taste. Refrigerate one hour before serving.

170 kcal Per Serving (makes 6) / Fat: 0.2g / Carbohydrates: 38.5g / Fiber: 6.1g / Protein: 4.7g

---

- Grab a couple of the poppers in a bag to take with you while you run out the door. They make a great snack that will stick with you a little longer than crackers and a piece of fruit. The garlic and cilantro bring plenty of flavor while the poblano peppers add just a little kiss of heat.

- This sweet potato salad is a tasty alternative to traditional potato salad and is loaded with fiber. Serve alongside any type of barbeque or grilled meat.

Tailgating Brisket Sliders

4 lb	brisket (excess fat trimmed)
	Himalayan pink salt and freshly ground pepper
2 Tbs	olive oil
6 oz	tomato paste
1 Tbs	dijon mustard
2 c	vegetable broth
3	red onions, quartered
5-6 cloves	garlic, pressed
3	carrots, peeled and sliced
2 Tbs	apple cider vinegar
2 Tbs	coconut liquid aminos
3	bay leaves
1 pkg	Hawaiian Rolls, cut crosswise

Sprinkle brisket on each side with salt and pepper. Heat oil in a large skillet and cook on each side until brisket is browned. Remove from pan. Set aside.

Warm tomato paste in pan for approximately 2-3 minutes. Then add 1 c of vegetable broth and mustard to make the liquid for the slow cooker. Put brisket and liquid in slow cooker and add remaining vinegar, aminos, vegetables and bay leaves and mix together. Cook brisket on low for 8 hours.

Remove the brisket and pull apart to sandwich between Hawaiian rolls to make sliders. Pull apart individual sliders and enjoy! Use liquid for an optional dipping sauce if desired.

415 kcal Per Serving (makes 16) / Fat: 26g / Carbohydrate: 21.3g / Fiber: 2.1g / Protein: 25.4g

- All you need is a good brisket, a crockpot and a few fresh, healthy ingredients and you're on your way to fun eating! Combine this with our original tailgating coleslaw made with broccoli, carrots, apples and cranberries and enjoy!

Chocolate Chili

3 lbs	fresh ground turkey
2 Tbs	coconut oil (divided)
1 1/2 c	yellow onion, chopped
3 cloves	garlic, minced
4 oz	green chilies
1/2 tsp	red pepper flakes
2 Tbs	chili powder
2 tsp	cumin
1 1/2 Tbs	coconut sugar
2 tsp	oregano
28 oz	chopped tomatoes
6 oz	tomato paste
8 oz	red wine (optional)
2	15 oz cans dark kidney beans
1 bar	Trader Joe's Dark Chocolate
1 tbs	cinnamon

Heat large skillet and stock pot with 1 Tbs coconut oil. In each pan, split turkey, onion and garlic. Saute contents in each pan until brown. Transfer all of the turkey mixture into the stock pot. Add in green chilies and cumin. Mix thoroughly and cook for 3 minutes. Add coconut sugar, dark chocolate bar and cook for 45 minutes. To finish this amazing dish off add your cinnamon and simmer for 5 minutes.

378 kcal Per Serving (makes 10) / Fat: 15.2g / Carbohydrate: 34.6g / Fiber: 8.8g / Protein: 31.6g

Our clients and friends, Maynie and Samantha Alvarez decided to play around with our Totality recipe and created an award-winning chili! It just reiterates what we always say about mixing it up and finding your next amazing creation. This creative duo added a tablespoon of Chipotle chili powder, one chopped jalapeno pepper and a few ounces of Death by Coconut Beer they found On Tap at Corks in Knoxville in lieu of the wine. Look where it led!!!

- We had fun creating a twist in a popular American classic. We got creative with dark chocolate which is rich in the antioxidants and paired it with spices so the two would have a nice balance.

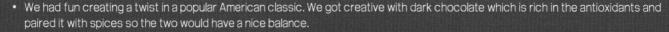

Chocolate Chili

Cranberry Quinoa

1 c	red quinoa
2 c	water
1/2 c	dried cranberries
1/3 c	sliced almonds
dash	salt

Put quinoa in a medium sauce pan. Add water and salt. Bring to a boil. Reduce heat to a simmer and boil for approximately 35 minutes. Add cranberries about halfway through. Stir in almonds once water has disappeared. Then serve!

272 kcal Per Serving (makes 4) / Fat: 8.6g / Carbohydrate: 42.6g / Fiber: 5g / Protein: 8.3g

- Quinoa has been listed as a perfect food because it includes healthy proteins, carbs and fats. Teamed with antioxidants from cranberries, you could say this is a complete dish. This Totality original was created specifically for one of our clients and the news covered Scott making it in our client's kitchen.

One Pot Cajun Quinoa and Turkey Dinner

1 1/2 c	quinoa, cooked according to package directions
1 lb	lean ground turkey (preferably 97% fat free)
3	bell peppers, sliced (any color will be fine)
1/2 c	fresh peas
1	carrot, chopped
1/2	medium onion, chopped
1	large tomato, chopped
3 cloves	garlic, minced
15 oz	crushed San Marzano Tomatoes
3 Tbs	tomato paste
1 Tbs	extra virgin olive oil
1 tsp	paprika
2 sprigs	fresh thyme
1 tsp	salt
1/2 tsp	cayenne pepper (optional)
1/2 tsp	dried oregano
1/2 tsp	red pepper flakes
1/4 tsp	fresh cracked black pepper

In a large skillet over medium heat, brown the ground turkey then drain and transfer to a bowl. Add the olive oil to the same skillet place over medium heat, then add the onion, carrot, peppers and cook for 3-4 minutes. After 3-4 minutes, add garlic and tomato paste along with all the spices. Let the tomato mixture cook for an additional 5 minutes over medium heat, or until the vegetables are softened; add the ground turkey, crushed tomatoes, cooked quinoa, and fresh peas. Continue to cook, stirring occasionally, until everything is heated through and the peas are done, then serve. If desired, add a few dashes of hot sauce for an additional kick.

325 kcal Per Serving (makes 4) / Fat: 3.2g / Carbohydrate: 40g / Fiber: 7.6g / Protein: 33.5g

• Weeknights are busy times and most of us would like a quick and healthy recipe to put together in a short amount of time without using a sink full of pots and pans. Aside from pre-cooking the quinoa, this dish takes less than 30 minutes to cook and keeps the dirty dishes to a minimum. The cajun spice and red pepper flakes are a fun twist and rev up the metabolism.

Carne Asada with Plantains

Carne Asada with Plantains

Carne Asada

3/4 c	orange juice, fresh squeezed
1/3 c	lime juice, fresh squeezed
4 cloves	garlic, minced
1/2 c	coconut liquid aminos
1 Tbs	chili powder
1 Tbs	cumin
1 Tbs	black pepper
1/2 c	olive oil
3 lbs	flank steak
1	red bell pepper, julienned
1	medium white onion, sliced into strips

Combine ingredients, whisk together, pour over meat and refrigerate overnight in a large bowl. Remove from marinade and saute over medium-high heat with sliced red bell pepper and onion strips for approximately 5-7 minutes on each side.

Sauteed Plantains

4	plantains, brown to black
1/2 c	coconut oil
1 Tbs	cinnamon

Cut the ends of the plantains off and then peel. Slice each plantain in half. Cut each half into 3 lengthwise slices. Melt oil in skillet on medium-high heat. Place plantain pieces into skillet and let them cook until the center pieces begin to darken on underneath side. Periodically check underneath side with a fork. Turn pieces over to finish cooking. Plantains are done when the centers are a rich golden brown. Remove with tongs onto a plate and sprinkle with cinnamon.

450 kcal Per Serving (makes 8) / Fat: 16.3g / Carbohydrate: 43.1g / Fiber: 2.6g / Protein: 38.1g

- Carne Asada is a Latin American dish that literally means grilled steak and plantains are tropical fruits that hold up well during cooking. They are similar to bananas in both appearance and in flavor. A green to yellow plantain is starchy like a potato and holds up well in frying or boiling. When the plantain is yellow to brown, it has a slight fruitiness and firm texture that suits any part of the meal. In this recipe we took plantains that are near black in color for their sweeter flavors to accompany the spices of the marinade in the steak. Black plantains are also ideal for dessert dishes. We learned firsthand how to cook plantains from the natives in the kitchen of a Costa Rican restaurant!

Cuban-style Beef and Peppers

1/4 c	raisins
1/4 c	white rum
1 lb	tri tip steak
2 Tbs	olive oil
3 c onion, thinly sliced	
1 c	yellow pepper, cut into strips
1	jalapeno, sliced
5 colves	garlic, minced
1/4 tsp	dried thyme
2 tsp	cumin
6	pimento stuffed green olives, chopped
3	plum tomatoes, cut into wedges
1 1/2 c	black rice

Combine raisins and rum in a bowl. Set aside for 30 minutes. Cut steak into thin strips. Cook rice and set aside. Heat oil in a large skillet. Add onions, yellow pepper, jalapeno and saute until tender. Add steak and garlic. Saute until browned (approximately 4 minutes). Add raisin mix, thyme, cumin, olives and tomatoes. Simmer until steak is done. Serve over rice.

475 kcal Per Serving (makes 5) / Fat: 13.3g / Carbohydrate: 61.6g / Fiber: 5.3g / Protein: 27.3g

• Take a culinary trip to Cuba with this exquisite dish. Loaded with flavor and healthy ingredients, this dish proves that healthy food can also taste amazing.

Beef and Butternut Squash Stew

2 lbs	lean stew beef, cut into 2-inch cubes
3 Tbs	olive oil
1	onion, peeled and chopped
2 cloves	garlic, chopped
1 lb	butternut squash, trimmed, and cut into 2-inch cubes
6 oz	mushrooms, sliced
3 c	low sodium beef broth
1/2 c	red wine
1 Tbs	fresh rosemary, minced
1 Tbs	fresh thyme, minced
1/4 c	sun-dried tomatoes, chopped
1/4 c	grated parmesan
1/2 tsp	salt, plus more to taste
	freshly ground black pepper to taste

In a large soup pot, heat 2 Tbs of olive oil over medium heat. Add beef cubes to the pot and cook for 5 minutes, or until beef is browned. Transfer the beef to a bowl and set aside. Add the remaining 1 Tbs of olive oil to the pot then add the onion, mushrooms, garlic, rosemary, and thyme. Saute over medium heat for 2-3 minutes. Add the red wine and gently stir for 1-2 minutes. Add the beef back to the pot along with the butternut squash and sun-dried tomatoes; stir to combine. Add enough broth to cover the beef and squash, which will be between 3-4 c. Bring the stew to a boil, then reduce the heat, cover and simmer over low heat for 1 hour. Right before serving, season the stew with additional salt and pepper to taste. Garnish each serving with parmesan.

380 kcal Per Serving (makes 5) / Fat: 13.6g / Carbohydrate: 15.3g / Fiber: 3.3g / 46.9g protein

• This warming stew is both rich in protein and antioxidants. Butternut squash is an exceptionally heart-friendly vegetable.

Tuscan Chicken Sandwich

4	bread loaves of your choice (approximately 4 inch long hoagie or artisan loaves)
16 oz	chicken cutlets
4 Tbs	olive oil, divided
1/4 c	balsamic vinegar
1	red pepper
1	portabella mushroom
3 sprigs	fresh rosemary
1/2 c	sundried tomatoes
1/3 c	Kalamata olives
1-3 cloves	garlic, crushed
	salt and pepper taste

Preheat stovetop pan or grill to medium high. Marinate chicken for 15 minutes in 2 Tbs of olive oil and balsamic vinegar. Combine rosemary, sundried tomatoes and olive oil in pan. Saute for 3 minutes. Set aside. Cut vegetables into strips and toss with 1 Tbs of olive oil and a pinch of salt and pepper. Grill chicken and vegetables. Slice chicken. Hollow out rolls leaving room to fill bread shell with fillings. Spread rolls with crushed garlic, and fill with chicken, vegetables, and top with rosemary mixture.

Enjoy your Tuscan creation!

466 kcal Per Serving (makes 4) / Fat: 21.3g / Carbohydrate: 45.4g / Fiber: 3.3g / Protein: 35g

* The flavors of summertime include many fresh vegetables and herbs. We've taken the basics and merged them together with a little Tuscan flair. Our Summertime Tuscan Chicken Sandwich is loaded with flavor and is as flavorful as it is colorful. Any small baguette or hoagie roll will work. We carved out the bread on the inside to make room for all of the delicious fillings which include chicken breast tender cutlets, marinated balsamic vinegar, olive oil, salt and pepper. This is a great way to eliminate excess carbs from the meal. The marinade is the finishing touch that makes this sandwich.

Tuscan Chicken Sandwich

Ultimate Chicken Soup

1 Tbs	olive oil
1 c	onion, diced
2 Tbs	chili powder
1 Tbs	orange rind, grated
1 Tsp	red pepper
7 cloves	garlic
2 c	cooked chicken
42 oz	chicken broth
2 c	red pepper, cut into strips
1/3 c	carrots, sliced
1/2 c	orange juice
2	limes, juiced
2 Tbs	jalapeno pepper, seeded and diced
4 c	cabbage, chopped
4 c	vegetable juice
2 c	cooked wild rice
1 Tbs	chili powder
6	roma tomatoes
3 cans	cannellini Beans

Bake chicken at 450 F or 20 minutes. Cool and shred and coat with lime juice. Heat oil in skillet and saute onion and garlic until tender. Add 1 can of broth and stir in all peppers. Cook for 15 minutes, stir in orange juice and put into a large stock pot. Add remaining broth, cabbage, vegetable juice, rice, chili powder and tomatoes. Bring to a boil and reduce to a simmer for 55 minutes. Add chicken, remaining beans and cook for 5 more minutes. Serve and enjoy!

512 kcal Per Serving (makes 6) / Fat: 8.9g / Carbohydrate: 74.3g / Fiber: 15.5g / Protein: 38.7g

- Our soup contains ingredients that are both healing and immune-boosting. Not only that, it is very balanced with protein, healthy carbs and many enzyme-rich vegetables. Soups are a convenient dish for any occasion. This soup is good alone or can be paired with a salad and bread for a fuller meal.

Chicken and Barley Stew with Kale and Sage

2 lb	skinless, boneless chicken breast, cut into 1 1/2 inch pieces
3 Tbs	olive oil
2	shallots, diced
1	carrot, peeled and diced
5 c	kale, chopped
2 cloves	garlic
1/4 c	sherry wine
1 Tbs	fresh sage, chopped
1/2 tsp	fresh thyme
1 3/4 c	pearled barley
5 c	low sodium chicken stock
1/2 - 1 c	water (depending on desired thickness)
1/4 c	almonds, sliced and roasted
	salt and pepper to taste

In a large soup pot, heat 2 Tbs of oil. Add the chicken and cook over medium high heat until slightly golden brown, about 2 minutes per side. Transfer the chicken to a bowl. Add the remaining 1 Tbs of olive oil along with the carrots to the pot and cook over medium-high heat for 3 minutes. Add shallots, garlic, sage, and thyme and cook for an additional 2 minutes. Deglaze the pan with the sherry, stirring constantly for 1 minutes. After most of the sherry is evaporated, add the chicken stock and pearled barley. Bring the stew to a boil then cover and simmer until the barley is almost done, about 25-30 minutes. Return the browned chicken breast to the stew along with the kale and simmer for an additional 10 minutes. Add salt and pepper to taste along with water if a thinner stew is desired. Spoon the stew into bowls then garnish with the sliced almond.

432 kcal Per Serving (makes 6) / Fat: 12.9g / Carbohydrate: 49.6g / Fiber: 9.9g / Protein: 36g

- Whole grain barley has some impressive health benefits. It is rich in vitamins and minerals and is very high in dietary fiber. Sage is a natural antiseptic with remarkable bacteria-killing abilities.

Chicken Fajitas with Zesty Guacamole

2	boneless, skinless chicken breast, sliced into strips
1 c	black beans, cooked and rinsed
2	bell peppers (preferably red and yellow), sliced
1/2	red onion, sliced
3 cloves	garlic
2 tsp	coconut oil, separated
2	avocados, seeded and peeled
1	lime, juiced
1 medium	tomato, diced
1/4	sweet onion, diced
1 Tbs	cilantro, chopped
2 tsp	chili powder
1 tsp	salt
1 tsp	paprika
1/2 tsp	onion powder
1/2 tsp	garlic powder
1/2 tsp	ground cumin
1/2 tsp	cayenne pepper

Begin by mixing salt, paprika, onion powder, garlic powder, ground cumin, and cayenne in a small bowl. Heat a skillet over medium heat, add one tsp of the coconut oil along with the chicken breast, and sprinkle half of the seasoning over the chicken. Saute the chicken for 8-10 minutes while turning occasionally. Once cooked, transfer the chicken to a bowl and set aside. Heat the skillet over medium heat once more with the remaining coconut oil. Add the bell peppers, red onion, and half of the diced tomato to the skillet. Sprinkle the remaining seasoning mixture over the vegetables and cook for 5 minutes. After 5 minutes, add 2 of the diced garlic cloves and cooked black beans, and cook for another 3-4 minutes. Once the vegetables are done, add the cooked chicken back to the skillet, and take the skillet off of the heat.

For the guacamole, place the avocados in a bowl and roughly mash with a fork; then add the remaining tomato, sweet onion, cilantro, lime juice, and remaining garlic clove. Stir to combine and add salt and pepper to taste. Serve the fajitas with shredded lettuce, a few lime wedges, salsa, and extra cilantro if desired.

410 kcals Per Serving / Fat: 16.7g / Carbohydrate: 22.2g / Fiber: 10g / Protein: 44.5g

- Chicken Fajitas aren't always the most calorie friendly option. This recipe delivers all of the flavor of traditional fajitas without the unnecessary calories so you can enjoy your own healthy Tex-Mex inspired dish!

Healthy Spaghetti

2 lbs	extra lean ground turkey
2 Tbs	extra-virgin coconut oil
1 pkg	brown rice quinoa spaghetti
10	large button mushrooms, sliced
18 oz	marinara sauce
1 c	fresh oregano, chopped
	Himalayan pink salt
	fresh ground pepper
1 tsp	dried minced onion
1 tsp	garlic powder

Bring water in a large stock pot to a boil with a dash of olive oil and Himalayan pink salt. Add spaghetti and boil according to package directions. Meanwhile, saute ground turkey with coconut oil, salt, pepper, garlic, and onion. Adjust according to taste. When turkey is browned, add mushrooms and oregano. Add marinara and bring mixture to a simmer. Drain pasta, add half of marinara mixture and toss together. Plate spaghetti and top each serving with 1 c of marinara mixture and fresh oregano. Enjoy!

442 kcals Per Serving (makes 5) / Fat: 9.5g / Carbohydrate: 48.5g / Fiber: 4.7g / Protein: 46.8g

- This spaghetti has been a huge hit among our clients and with viewers who saw it on the Knoxville ABC affiliate, WATE-TV. The quinoa, brown rice noodles are gluten-free and the ground turkey is low fat. That makes for a win-win dish! (We found our noodles at Trader Joe's).

Springtime Shrimp Kabob

Springtime Shrimp Kabob

12	large shrimp, peeled
2	large Fuji apples, cubed
1	large jicama, cubed
1	jalapeno pepper, sliced
1/4 c	grapeseed oil
1 Tbs	cumin
4	medium bamboo or metal skewers
3/4 c	mayonnaise or plain fat free Greek Yogurt
1/4 c	pineapple juice
1 Tbs	sriracha hot sauce
1 Tbs	coconut sugar

In a large bowl, combine shrimp, apple, jicama, oil cumin and cayenne. Mix together and place in refrigerator to marinate for 30 minutes. Remove and place items on skewers alternating shrimp, apple, jicama and jalapeno (as preferred). Place over a heat source of choice and evenly cook all sides until shrimp is thoroughly cooked with a rich pink tone. Set aside.

In a mixing bowl combine mayonnaise/yogurt, pineapple juice, sriracha and coconut sugar and whisk until thoroughly blended into a liquid. Lightly drizzle over the kabobs and serve.

345 kcal Per Serving (makes 4) / Fat: 14.3g / Carbohydrate: 37.7 / Fiber: 17.2g / Protein: 19.2g

• Consider cooking our kabobs on a large Himalayan pink salt block. Himalayan pink salt is growing in popularity from lamps to table salt. This prehistoric rock is also great to cook on and provides many benefits: a salty addition to foods, rich in minerals, easy to clean and great as a decorative serving platter. They only need to be rinsed because of their antimicrobial nature and are a fun way to jazz up things in the kitchen.

Big Daddy BBQ with Sweet Potato Fries

Big Daddy BBQ with Sweet Potato Fries

BBQ

5 Tbs	coconut sugar, divided
3/4 tsp	black pepper
2 1/2 lbs	turkey breast filets
1 c	chopped onion
1 c	tomato paste
3 Tbs	Worcestershire sauce
3 Tbs	molasses
3 Tbs	apple cider vinegar
1 Tbs	chili powder
1 tsp	garlic powder
1 tsp	dry mustard
1 tsp	ground cumin
1/2 tsp	Himalayan pink salt
	sandwich rolls
	red diced onion (optional)
	sliced dill pickles (optional)

Combine 1 Tbs coconut sugar and pepper; rub over both sides of turkey breast filets. Combine 1/4 c coconut sugar, onion, and the remaining ingredients in an electric crock pot. Add turkey; turn to coat. Cover with lid and cook on high for 1 hour. Reduce heat setting to low and cook for 4 hours. Remove turkey and reserve sauce. Lightly shred turkey breasts in a food processor and return to crock pot with sauce. Stir and spoon BBQ mixture on rolls and top with desired optional items.

Sweet Potato Fries

4	large sweet potatoes
3 Tbs	olive oil
1 Tbs	dried Italian seasonings
1/2 tsp	garlic powder
	Himalayan pink salt (to taste)

Heat oven to 350 F. Peel and slice potatoes into 1/4 inch wedges. Place them into a bowl and coat them thoroughly with olive oil using hands. Spread over 1-2 cookie sheets and sprinkle with seasonings, garlic and salt and bake for 1 hour. Turn them with a spatula every 20 minutes to ensure even baking. Finally, broil on high for 5 minutes to achieve a mild crispy texture. Let cool slightly and serve.

Macros does not include the bun.

346 kcal Per Serving (makes 8) / Fat: 6.6g / Carbohydrate: 41.5g / Fiber: 4.4g / Protein: 29g

- Here we have a healthier BBQ option and created this recipe to take care of Dad's heart in honor of Father's Day. The protein count is high, the fat is low and it's easily digested. There is nothing processed or artificial in our sauce. The molasses is loaded with iron and Vitamin B. The chili powder is a metabolic booster and the garlic is a great anti-viral component. Apple cider vinegar adds a richer, less acidic flavor and aids in digestion. These simple fries contain dietary fiber and stabilize blood sugar after a meal and help you feel fuller longer after eating.

Chicken-Turkey Wraps and Pumpkin Waffles

Turkey

1 1/4 lb	chicken breast strips
1 pkg	uncured turkey bacon
	Salt and pepper to taste
	cooking spray
	foil
6-12	toothpicks

Preheat oven to 450 F. Line casserole dish with foil and lightly coat with cooking spray. Fully wrap each chicken strip completely with a piece of turkey bacon and place in casserole dish in rows and sprinkle with desired amount of pepper and a light dash of salt if desired (the bacon will provide saltiness). Place in oven and bake for 20 minutes. Remove dish from oven and gently pierce each wrap with a toothpick to keep the bundled wrap together. Remove individual wraps with tongs and plate over waffles when ready to serve. Top with a Totality chutney. We suggest the Apple-Cranberry Chutney.

Pumpkin Waffles

1 1/2 c	pre-packaged pancake mix (we used Pamela's Gluten-free Baking and Pancake Mix)
2 Tbs	pumpkin pie spice
2	large eggs
2 Tbs	maple syrup
1/4 tsp	vanilla extract
3/4 c	almond milk
1 Tbs	coconut oil, melted
3/4 c	canned pumpkin

Begin by first mixing pancake mix and pumpkin pie spice together. Create a well in the center of dry mixture and add eggs, maple syrup, vanilla, almond milk and oil. Stir together just until moist and then mix in pumpkin. Pour batter onto hot, lightly sprayed waffle maker, close and cook until waffles are done. Repeat until all batter has been used.

373 kcal Per Serving (makes 6) / Fat: 14.4g / Carbohydrate: 28.9g / Fiber: 2g / Protein: 32.6g

- We enjoy taking traditional dishes, especially comfort foods and like to tweak them to add an element of healthy flair. The lean protein in this dish replaces the fried chicken and the added pumpkin puree added to the waffles still packs a punch of flavor. With these changes you get less fat and tons of antioxidants. The gravy is replaced with one of our delicious chutneys!

Chicken-Turkey Wraps and Pumpkin Waffles

Apple-Cranberry Chutney

3 c	apple, peeled and diced
1/2 c	tart dried cranberries (canned may be used as a substitute)
1/4 c	balsamic vinegar
1/3 c	water
2 Tbs	coconut sugar
1/2 tsp	ground ginger

Combine all ingredients in sauce pan. Bring to a boil. Cover. Reduce heat. Simmer for 20 minutes until fruit is tender.

126 kcal Per Serving (makes 4) / Fat: 0.2g / Carbohydrate: 33g / Fiber: 3.2g / Protein: 0.2g

Southern Peach Chutney

1 Tbs	olive oil
1/2 c	red pepper, diced
1/2 c	red onion, diced
3 cloves	garlic, minced
1/2	jalapeno pepper, diced
2	peaches, peeled and sliced
2 Tbs	coconut sugar
2 Tbs	red wine vinegar

Oil a skillet and combine pepper, onion, garlic and jalapeno and saute until softened. Stir in peaches, sugar, vinegar and simmer for 20 minutes. Remove and let sit until cool. Refrigerate unused portions.

88 kcal Per Serving (makes 4) / Fat: 3.6g / Carbohydrate: 14.4g / Fiber: 1.5g / Protein: 1g

Sweet and Savory Balsamic Sauce

1 tsp	olive oil
3 cloves	garlic, crushed
1/4 c	onion, minced
3 Tbs	balsamic vinegar
2 Tbs	fresh rosemary, finely chopped
2 Tbs	fresh sage, finely chopped
2 Tbs	fresh thyme, finely chopped
1/4 c	white wine
1/2 c	chicken broth
2 tsp	honey
1/2 tsp	cornstarch

- Our chutneys provide delicious taste and can add unique flavor to any meal. In fact, they can make the most ordinary meal extraordinary.

In a large skillet heat olive oil. Add onion, garlic and fresh herbs. Saute until flavors are infused. Then add wine and broth and bring to a boil. Reduce heat. Simmer uncovered until mixture reduces to approximately 1/3 of a c. In a separate bowl combine honey and cornstarch and add to broth mixture. Bring to a boil and cook for 1 minute and constantly stir. Serve over your favorite lean protein.

25 kcal Per Serving (makes 5) / Fat: 1g / Carbohydrate: 3.5g / Fiber: 0g / Protein: 0.6g

Santa Fe Orange-Chipotle Sauce

2 Tbs	olive oil
1 c	onion chopped
1 c	tomato chopped
3 Tbs	garlic, minced
3 Tbs	chopped, drained canned chipotle chilies in adobo sauce
2 c	orange juice
1 c	white balsamic vinegar
1/2 c	tomato paste
1/4 c	coconut sugar
1/4 c	molasses
	salt and pepper to taste
1/4 c	freshly squeezed lime juice
1/2 c	cilantro, chopped

Heat oil in large skillet. Add onions and saute for 10 minutes or until lightly brown. Add tomatoes, garlic, and chilies and cook for 3 minutes. Add orange juice and vinegar. Bring to a boil. Reduce heat and simmer until reduced to approximately 1 1/2 c (around 30 minutes). Stir in tomato paste, sugar, molasses, salt and pepper. Cook for 5 minutes. Put mixture into a blender and blend until smooth. Stir in cilantro and lime juice.

101 kcal per serving (makes 14) / Fat: 2.1g / Carbohydrate: 19.7g / Fiber: 1g / Protein: 1g

Tropical Mango Chutney

3 c	mango, peeled and diced
1/2 c	golden raisins
1/4 c	apple cider vinegar
1/3 c	coconut water
2 Tbs	coconut sugar
1 tsp	ground ginger

Combine all ingredients in a saucepan. Bring to a boil. Cover and reduce heat to a simmer and cook for 20 minutes or until fruit is tender.

53 kcal Per Serving (makes 6) / Fat: 0.03g / Carbohydrate: 14g / Fiber: 1.3g / Protein: 0.7g

- The fruits and vegetables in our chutneys along the with the many spices and herbs add a beneficial nutritional component which can aid the digestive system.

Michelle's Breakfast Banana Split

1 c	oatmeal (we used Trader Joe's Gluten Free Rolled Oats)
1 c	fresh blueberries
1 c	fresh sliced strawberries
2	bananas (vertically sliced and then cut into halves)
1 c	vanilla Greek yogurt
1 c	dark chocolate morsels
1 c	chopped walnuts (or any other chopped nuts)
	honey (to taste)

Arrange 2 banana slices evenly at the sides of each bowl. Prepare oatmeal to label directions, then divide evenly into bottom of bowls as a base. Top with a 1/4 c of vanilla yogurt and remaining toppings. Drizzle desired amount of honey to taste on top and enjoy!

676 kcal Per Serving (makes 4) / Fat: 41.4g / Carbohydrate: 76.3 / Fiber: 11.8g / Protein: 13g

- We are excited to share a dish that will have your kids and anyone else in your family ready to eat their breakfast! Breakfast is a meal that is very important to include in our day, however, many people overlook it. It provides, energy, mental clarity and regulates our metabolism. Our Breakfast Banana Split provides essential nutrients, fiber and a ton of flavor. Cooked oatmeal is our base. Along with that, we've added banana which is rich in potassium, strawberries which contain vitamin C, blueberries which are high in antioxidants, a dollop of vanilla Greek yogurt which provides calcium, and to top it off, a few morsels of dark chocolate and some chopped walnuts. Dark chocolate isn't as high in sugar as milk chocolate and contains antioxidants as well. Walnuts provide a healthy source of fats to the brain and those good fats help with concentration and memory.

Michelle's Breakfast Banana Split

Protein Pancakes

2 c	old fashioned rolled oats
1 c	fat free Greek yogurt
4	large egg whites
2 Tbs	pumpkin puree
2 Tbs	almond milk
2 tsp	vanilla extract
1 tsp	baking soda
1/2 tsp	salt

Begin by placing oats in a food processor and blend until the oats are a flour-like consistency. Add the oat flour, baking soda, and salt to a large bowl and whisk. Add the Greek yogurt, egg whites, almond milk, pumpkin puree, and vanilla to the oat flour mixture and combine. Heat a skillet over medium heat and spray with non-stick cooking spray. Add the batter 1/2 c at a time to the heated pan and cool for 3-4 minutes per side, or until golden brown.

215 kcal Per Serving (makes 4) / Fat: 3.1g / Carbohydrate: 31.1g / Fiber: 4.4g / Protein: 16g

• These creative pancakes were created by our awesome staff member, Jesse Johnson. He creatively threw together a protein masterpiece by adding flavorful ingredients. Not only that, these rock and keep you feeling full with all of the hearty fiber. For an even bigger protein punch try pairing these with chicken-apple sausage or a bacon variety.

Strawberry and Lemon Compote

1 c	strawberries, diced
1	lemon, zested and juiced
1/4 c	honey
1/2 tsp	vanilla extract
3	mint leaves, chopped

In a separate sauce pan over medium heat, combine diced strawberries, lemon juice and zest, honey, and vanilla. Cook over medium heat for abound 5 minutes, stirring occasionally. Just before serving, add the chopped mint leaves. Serve warm over the pancakes.

81 kcal Per Serving (makes 4) / Fat: 0g / Carbohydrate: 19.75g / Fiber: 0.5g / Protein: 0.25g

Olympic Ring Oatmeal

Olympic Ring Oatmeal

1/2 c	Trader Joe's Gluten Free Rolled Oats
1/2 c	fresh blueberries (Blue Ring)
1 tsp	chia seeds (Black Ring)
1/4 c	dried goji berries (Red Ring)
1 Tbs	honey (Yellow Ring)
1	medium granny smith apple, cubed (Green Ring)
dash	of cinnamon to taste
2 Tbs	coconut oil
1/4 c	almond milk (adjust for desired consistency)

Pre-cook the oats according to package directions and set aside. Saute apple and goji berries in skillet on medium heat with coconut oil and cinnamon. Cook until slightly softened. Add this mixture to cooked oatmeal. Then add remaining ingredients and stir in desired amount of almond milk.

Enjoy this heart-healthy and performance based meal!

600 Kcal Per Serving (makes 1) / Fat: 20.3 / Carbohydrate: 101.6g / Fiber: 16.2g / Protein: 11.25g

• This hearty oatmeal dish is great for for athletes of all ages and will kick your energy into high gear!

Caribbean Coconut Sundae

4 Tbs	coconut oil
4	bananas peeled and sliced in half
4 Tbs	coconut sugar
2 tsp	cinnamon
2 tsp	vanilla
1/4 c	molasses
1 Tbs	pineapple juice
4	large scoops coconut gelato

In a large skillet melt 2 Tbs coconut oil on medium heat. Add bananas and saute until browned on both sides. Set aside. Melt the other 2 Tbs of coconut oil in same skillet. Stir in coconut sugar, cinnamon, vanilla, molasses and pineapple juice. Add bananas back in and coat with sauce. Dish up bananas, top with gelato and drizzle with remaining sauce. That's how you create a quick healthy dessert that your whole family will enjoy!!

528 kcal Per Serving (makes 4) / Fat: 23.3g / Carbohydrate: 82.8g / Fiber: 4g / Protein: 4g

• This rich dessert is loaded with great flavor and health benefits. It includes bananas which are rich in potassium. Potassium regulates water balance and can help with bloating. Molasses is rich in iron and is a great sweetener for diabetics because it doesn't cause dangerous blood sugar spikes. Coconut sugar is low on the glycemic index as well and coconut oil is metabolism-boosting oil. Rounding this out are the spices cinnamon and vanilla.

Caribbean Coconut Sundae

Grilling Cuisine

Poolside Luau Boats

Poolside Luau Boats

2	large pineapples
1 lb	pork tenderloin
1 c	chopped pineapple
1 c	chopped mango
1 c	coarsely chopped red pepper
1 c	kiwi, cubed
3/4 c	red onion
1/3 c	cilantro, fresh minced
1 c	banana, chopped
2 Tbs	lime juice
1 Tbs	jalapeno, chopped with seeds removed
1	lime, juiced
1 Tbs	coconut sugar
1/3 c	liquid coconut aminos
dash	of salt and pepper
	coconut oil spray

Cut pineapple in half lengthwise. Use a small paring knife to make a cut about 1/2 - inch from pineapple skin (all the way around the pineapple). Remove core and discard that. Remove remaining carved out pineapple to save for salsa mixture and make sure to leave 1/2 inch of flesh in the pineapple boat. Wrap each pineapple crown in foil. Set the pineapple boat (shells) aside and chop the remaining pineapple. Whisk together lime juice, coconut sugar and liquid coconut aminos until sugar is dissolved. Pour over pork tenderloin in a large gallon sized freezer bag and let sit for 10 minutes to marinade.

Next, assemble remaining ingredients in a large mixing bowl (except for oil) to create the pineapple salsa. Set aside.

Grill pork for approximately for 20 minutes over medium-high heat until center is no longer pink. Cut pork into small pieces and add to the salsa mixture.

Spray pineapple shells with coconut oil spray and fill shells with the pork and salsa mixture. Add desired amount of salt and pepper. Put in oven and bake at 350 F for 10 minutes to enhance the flavors. Remove from oven and remove foil.

Serve your Luau Boats, put on your grass skirts, and enjoy your luau!

272 kcal Per Serving (makes 6) / Fat: 2.4g / Carbohydrate: 40.1g / Fiber: 4.2g / Protein: 30.5g

- These pineapple-filled boats are a hit whether you are on the patio, in the dining room or poolside. Pineapples have been used for centuries to treat indigestion and inflammation in both Central and South America. Bromelain is the enzyme found in pineapples used to treat these ailments.

Quick and Easy Herb Pizza Crust *use for any Totality grilled pizzas*

2 c	bread flour
1/2 tsp	salt
1/2 tsp	sugar
1 Tbs	dried rosemary
1 tsp	garlic powder
1 pkg	quick rise yeast
3/4 c	warm water (120-130 degrees)
1 Tbs	olive oil
2 Tbs	cornmeal

Combine flour, salt, sugar, rosemary, garlic and yeast in a large bowl. Make a well in the center of the mix and set aside. In a new bowl combine water and oil. Add to flour mix and stir until the mixture forms a ball. Turn dough out onto a floured surface and knead until smooth and elastic for approximately 10 minutes. Place the dough in a large bowl and coat it with cooking spray. Turn to coat and then cover and let rise in a warm draft-free area for approximately 40-45 minutes. Punch the dough down and then divide in half. Cover and let rise for 10 minutes. Working with one portion at a time, roll each portion into a 10 inch circle on a lightly floured surface. Place the dough on a baking sheets to shape and sprinkle each with 1 Tbs of cornmeal. Remove dough from sheets when ready to grill your favorite grilled Totality Pizza. Spray one side generously before placing on the grill.

Heat the grill to Low. Place the sprayed side of crust on hot grill. Cook for 3 minutes or until the crust puffs. Flip crust over. Brush with 1 Tbs of olive oil.

232 kcal Per Serving (makes 4) / Fat: 3.5g / Carbohydrate: 44.5g / Fiber: 0g / Protein: 8g

• This pizza basic is simple to make and kicks up the taste buds with rich herbs and is a hit with a variety of pizza toppings.

Prosciutto-Goat Cheese and Grilled Pepper Pizza

Prepare all grilled ingredients prior to building pizza

1 c	orange pepper, ring sliced
1 c	yellow pepper, ring sliced
1 c	red pepper, ring sliced
1 c	red onion, ring sliced
1 Tbs	olive oil
2	10" prepared crust (see Quick and Easy Herb Pizza Crust)
6 oz	prosciutto
4 oz	goat cheese, crumbled (room temperature)

Heat the grill to medium. Take all rings and put in a medium bowl add 1Tbs olive oil toss to coat. Put vegetables on grill cook until tender for approximately 10 mins. Set aside. Now you're ready to build your pizza. Turn the grill down to low. Spray one side generously before placing on the grill. Place the sprayed side of crust on hot grill. Cook for 3 minutes or until the crust puffs. Flip crust over. Brush with 1 Tbs of olive oil add half of your veggies, prosciutto and goat cheese. Close grill lid and cook for about 5 minutes or until cheese is moderately melted. Repeat process for second pizza with remaining ingredients.

460 kcal per serving (makes 4) / Fat: 17.5g / Carbohydrate: 56.4 / Fiber: 2g / Protein: 26.25

Grilled BBQ Pork Pizza

12 oz	grilled pork loin cut into chunks (precooked)
1 c	grilled sliced red onion
1 Tbs	olive oil
	salt and pepper
2/3 c	BBQ sauce
2	10" prepared crust (see Quick and Easy Herb Pizza Crust)
1 1/2 c	pineapple, fresh chopped
4 oz	jalapeno-jack cheese, sliced
4 oz	mozzarella cheese, sliced

Heat the grill to medium. In a medium bowl add onion & olive oil toss to coat add salt & pepper. Grill for about 5 minutes. Remove and set aside. In a large bowl, combine 1/3 c BBQ sauce, pork and mix together. Set aside. Now you're ready to build your pizza. Turn the grill down to low. Spray one side generously before placing on the grill. Place the sprayed side of crust on hot grill. Cook for 3 minutes or until the crust puffs. Flip crust over. Add half of remaining BBQ sauce and half of all ingredients. Cover grill cook for about 5 minutes or until cheese is melted. Repeat with second crust and remaining ingredients.

704 kcal Per Serving (makes 4) / Fat: 22.5g / Carbohydrate: 94.5g / Fiber: 1.4g / Protein: 39g

Grilled Veggie Pizza

3 Tbs	balsamic vinegar
4 cloves	garlic, crushed
1	eggplant, cut horizontally 1/4" thick
2 c	yellow squash, sliced
	salt & pepper
2	10" prepared crust (see Quick and Easy Herb Pizza Crust)
2 tsp	olive oil
2 c	chopped heirloom tomatoes
8 oz	feta, crumbled
1/2 c	parmesan cheese, shredded
1/4 c	fresh oregano
1 1/2 c	spinach, thinly sliced
2 Tbs	balsamic vinegar
1/2 Tbs	olive oil
	spicy red peppers (optional)

Heat the grill to medium. Combine 3 Tbs vinegar & garlic in small bowl brush over both sides of eggplant and yellow squash slices. Sprinkle with salt & pepper. Place eggplant on grill cook about 2min each side. Set aside. Now you're ready to build your pizza. Turn the grill down to low. Spray one side generously before placing on the grill. Place the sprayed side of crust on hot grill. Cook for 3 minutes or until the crust puffs. Flip crust over. Brush with 1 Tbs of olive oil and add half of eggplant, squash, tomatoes, cheeses and oregano. Cover and grill for approximately 4 minutes. Combine spinach, vinegar and olive oil. Top with half of the mixture. Sprinkle with peppers to taste. Repeat with second crust and remaining ingredients.

534 kcal Per Serving (makes 4) / Fat: 23.5g / Carbohydrate: 62.5g / Fiber: 5.6g / Protein: 23.7g

Grilled Mahi Mahi with Mango Salsa and Roasted Asparagus

4 6 oz	Mahi Mahi fillets
1/2 tsp	garlic salt
1 tsp	coconut oil, melted
3/4 c	mango, fresh diced
1/2 c	cucumber, diced
1	habanero pepper, seeded and diced
1	lime, juiced
1/2	bell pepper
2 lbs	fresh asparagus
1	lemon, sliced
1 tsp	olive oil
1/4 tsp	sea salt
	salt and pepper to taste

In a medium bowl, combine mango, cucumber, bell pepper, habanero, and lime juice. Toss together, season with salt to taste, and set aside in the refrigerator.

Preheat oven to 400 degrees and break off the tough ends of the asparagus. Place the asparagus on a baking sheet and drizzle with the oil olive then season with the sea salt. Once seasoned, place the lemon slices on top of the asparagus and place them in the oven. Roast for 25 minutes, or until the asparagus is crisp but still tender.

For the fish, begin by preheating the grill on medium-high heat. Brush each fillet with coconut oil and season each with garlic salt. Place fillets on heated grill and cook 4-5 minutes per side, only flipping once. Serve the fish topped with the mango salsa alongside the asparagus.

240 kcal Per Serving (makes 4) / Fat: 3.8g / Carbohydrate: 16g / Fiber: 5.6g / Protein: 37g

• Asparagus is an excellent water eliminator and helps control bloating. Mahi Mahi is a delicious and delicate fish with a very meaty texture and pairs perfectly with the sweet and spicy mango salsa. The citrus notes of the roasted asparagus are also a great compliment to the fish and is best paired with an Oceanside view!

Honey Sriracha Chicken with Brown Rice and Roasted Broccoli

1 lb	chicken breast (or tenders), boneless and skinless
1/3 c	Sriracha sauce
1/4 c	fat free buttermilk
2 Tbs	honey
1 c	brown rice
1 c	chicken stock
1 1/4 c	water
1/2 tsp	garlic powder
1 lb	broccoli florets (about 3 c)
2 tsp	sesame oil
2 cloves	garlic, minced
1 tsp	sesame seeds
1/2 tsp	salt
	black pepper to taste

Begin by marinating the chicken by placing it in an airtight container along with combining sriracha, buttermilk and honey. Marinate the chicken for at least 30 minutes and up to 2 hours. Preheat grill to medium-high, or oven to 375 degrees. After marinating, place on the grill, or on a baking sheet if using an oven, sprinkle with salt, and cook for 15-20 minutes. Flip the chicken halfway through the cooking time. After cooked, place the chicken on a plate to rest while the rest of the meal is prepared.

While the chicken cooks, start on the side dishes. For the brown rice, bring water, chicken stock, and garlic powder to a boil in a pot over medium heat. Once a boil is reached, add the rice, reduce the heat, cover and simmer for 30-40 minutes, or until rice is tender.

For the sesame broccoli, preheat oven to 425 degrees and lightly oil a baking sheet. In a large bowl, toss together broccoli, sesame oil, 1/2 tsp salt, and minced garlic. Once broccoli is completely coated, place on baking sheet and sprinkle with sesame seeds. Place in oven and bake for 7-10 minutes, or until broccoli is just lightly brown on the edges. Once cooked, plate broccoli on long side rice and place chicken atop the rice. Enjoy alongside extra sriracha if desired.

386 kcal Per Serving (makes 4) / Fat: 6.7g / Carbohydrate: 51.7g / Fiber: 1.1g / Protein: 32.5g

- Honey contains flavonoids and antioxidants, which make it an important component in helping it to boost the immune system. Try to buy locally grown honey when possible to help boost the immune system to local pollens. The buttermilk and Sriracha-honey combo may seem a little strange, but this blend works perfectly with chicken breasts in this delicious Asian-inspired dish.

Grilled Pork Tenderloin with Sweet Potatoes and Green Beans

Grilled Pork Tenderloin with Sweet Potatoes and Green Beans

1	pork tenderloin
1/4 c	dijon mustard
1/8 c	white wine (Pinot Grigio or Chardonnay)
3 sprigs	thyme
1 Tbs	black pepper
2 lbs	sweet potatoes, skins left on and chopped
2 Tbs	fresh rosemary, chopped
1 Tbs	coconut oil, melted
1/2 tsp	salt
1/2	lime, juiced
12 oz	green beans
2 cloves	garlic
2 tsp	olive oil

Begin by combining pork tenderloin, mustard, wine, thyme, and black pepper in an airtight container; marinate the pork for at least 30 minutes before grilling. While the pork is marinating, prep sweet potatoes and preheat the oven to 400 degrees. In a large bowl, toss the sweet potatoes with the melted coconut oil. Once coated, added the rosemary and salt to the potatoes and toss again. Arrange sweet potatoes on a greased baking sheet. Bake sweet potatoes for 30-40 minutes, or until slightly brown and tender.

While the sweet potatoes roast, preheat the grill to a medium-high heat. Remove the pork from the marinade and place on the heated grill. Continue to cook for 12-15 minutes with the lid closed, turning every 3-4 minutes, until the internal temperature reads 150 degrees. Once the correct internal temperature is reached, remove pork from the grill, and let it rest for 10 minutes before slicing and serving. Serve with extra dijon mustard if desired

While the pork rests, add the olive oil and green beans to a skillet over medium heat. Saute the green beans, stirring occasionally, for 8-10 minutes. After 8-10 minutes, add in the garlic and a healthy pinch of salt. Continue cooking for another 4-5 minutes. After green beans are done, plate the pork and sweet potatoes alongside them.

350 kcal Per Serving (makes 5) / Fat: 12.9g / Carbohydrate: 30.8g / Fiber: 6.1g / Protein: 25g

- When cooked right, pork tenderloin can be an extremely succulent piece of meat, and the combination of mustard and white wine help to bring loads of flavor while naturally tenderizing the meat.

Scott's BBQ Salmon and Strawberry Salad

4	6oz salmon fillets
1/2 c	pineapple juice
2 Tbs	lemon juice
4 tsp	lemon rind
2 Tbs	coconut sugar
3 tsp	chili powder
3/4 tsp	ground cumin
1/2 tea	cinnamon

Rinse fillets in cold water and pat dry. Combine pineapple, lemon juice, lemon rind and sugar with salmon fillets in zip-lock bag and marinate for at least 1 hr. Preheat oven to 400 degrees or grill. Discard marinade & place fish in a baking dish. Rub with chili powder, cumin, and cinnamon. Cook fish for 12 minutes or until fish can be flaked with a fork.

239 kcal Per Serving (makes 4) / Fat: 6g / Carbohydrate: 10.1g / Fiber: 0g / Protein: 35g

- Salmon is rich in heart-healthy omega 3 fatty acids. By making a BBQ rub, you can avoid some of the unwanted additives found in many store-bought rubs.

Scott's BBQ Salmon and Strawberry Salad

Strawberry Chicken Tacos with BBQ Sauce

Strawberry Chicken Tacos with BBQ Sauce

8	Ezekiel 4:9 Sprouted Whole Grain Tortillas
1 lb	chicken thighs
1/3 c	barbeque sauce
1 c	shredded monterey jack cheese
1 1/2 c	sliced strawberries
2 Tbs	Italian seasoning
1 tsp	garlic powder
	A drizzle of honey per taco

Marinate chicken in a bowl for 15 minutes with BBQ sauce. Place over a grill until done. Cut chicken and set aside.

Place cheese in equal amounts onto tortillas and warm them in oven on warm until cheese melts. Add chicken and strawberries and place back in the oven for 2 minutes. Remove and sprinkle with garlic powder and Italian seasoning. Drizzle with honey and enjoy this powerfully tasty taco!!

485 kcal Per Serving (makes 4) / Fat: 21g / Carbohydrate: 42g / Fiber: 4.8g / Protein: 32.4g

- Fruit is the wildcard in this recipe. When we think of taco dishes, we generally think of spices and cheese. The strawberries add an elegant sweetness and a hearty dose of vitamin C. The sprouted grain tacos are low carb and gluten-free.

Marinated Teriyaki Pork Tenderloin

1 Tbs	coconut oil
1 Tbs	brown sugar
2 Tbs	coconut liquid aminos
1 Tbs	dry sherry vinegar
1 Tbs	rice vinegar
1 clove	garlic, crushed with a garlic press or minced
1/2 tsp	finely grated fresh ginger
pinch	red pepper flakes
1 lb	pork tenderloin

Combine the oil, sugar, aminos, sherry vinegar, vinegar, garlic, ginger and red pepper flakes, and stir until the sugar dissolves. Transfer to a resealable plastic bag and add the pork tenderloin. Seal the bag and marinate the pork in the refrigerator, turning once, for 1/2 hour, or up to 8 hours. Preheat grill on medium heat. Place the pork on the grill for 25 minutes, turning once. Cook until internal temp is 160 F.

204 kcal (Makes 4) / Fat: 8.7g / Carbohydrate: 5.3g / Fiber: 2g / Protein: 22.3g

• Pork tenderloin always provides a great alternative to chicken. It is lean like chicken but gives a different texture and can be a tasty lean asset to any dish.

Marinated Teriyaki Pork Tenderloin

His and Her Salad with Tri-Tip and Lime Vinaigrette

His and Her Salad with Tri-Tip and Lime Vinaigrette

Marinate Tri-Tip Roast

16 oz	tri-tip roast
1/2 c	olive oil
1 tsp	garlic powder
1 tsp	onion powder
1 tsp	dried rosemary
1	lemon, juiced
	salt and pepper

Salad

4 c	fresh spinach
1/3 c	roasted pecans
1/2 c	feta cheese
3/4 c	fresh blackberries

Lime Vinaigrette

1/4 c	olive oil
1/4 c	balsamic vinegar
1/4 c	honey
2	limes, juiced
	Salt and pepper to taste

In a large bowl coat evenly with all ingredients and marinate for 1/2 hour in refrigerator. Bake Tri-Tip Roast at 425 F for 40 minutes. Mix oil, vinegar, honey, lime juice salt and pepper. Whisk together in bowl until blended. Assemble spinach and lime vinaigrette in mixing bowl and toss with tongs until evenly coated. Top with feta, berries, nuts and sliced steak.

440 kcal Per Serving (makes 2) / Fat: 23.6g / Carbohydrate: 21.6g / Fiber: 3g / Protein: 37g

- How many times have you and your significant other differed in what you crave for dinner? The His and Hers Salad offers one possible solution for those dinner dilemmas when one might want heavier foods such as meat, cheese and nuts while the other may want something on the lighter, more refreshing side. This unique blend provides an adequate amount of substantial protein, healthy omega 3 fats, antioxidants, iron and fiber.

Culinary Creations by the UT Culinary Department

Our friends at the University of Tennessee Culinary Department were kind enough to create some special dishes for our first Taste of Totality cookbook. Chef Greg Eisele C.E.C., oversees the department and Michelle has the honor of regularly teaching the healthy cooking class in his program. While a bit more advanced than traditional Totality recipes, these delicious creations are from their 2016 Culinary Program Students. We encourage you to give them a try

Herb Seared Scallops with Artichoke Relish and Sunflower Risotto

Presented by Chef Greg Eisele C.E.C. and 2016 Culinary Program Students, Rosa D'Jara Rivers and Jacquie Ann Crochet

Scallops

3 oz	extra virgin olive oil
2 tsp	thyme, fresh fine chopped
2 tsp	dill, fresh fine chopped
1 Tbs	parsley, fine chopped
1 Tbs	cajun seasoning
4	large sea scallops, fresh 12-15 per lb

Relish

2 c	artichoke quarters, small diced
2 oz	green onion, fine chopped
2 Tbs	roasted red peppers, small diced
1 Tbs	lemon juice
1 Tbs	garlic, roasted minced
2 Tbs	fresh fennel, roasted small diced
2 Tbs	extra virgin olive oil

Sunflower Risotto

12 oz	sunflower seeds, shelled
8 oz	chicken stock
8 oz	heavy cream
4 Tbs	green onion, chopped
1 Tbs	sea salt
2 tsp	black pepper
4 oz	gruyere cheese

Garnish

1 Tbs	fresh lemon zests
4 sprigs	fresh thyme
4	carrot peelings razor thin
2 Tbs	micro greens

Combine olive oil thru cajun spice to make scallop marinade. Marinate scallops for 1 hour. Reserve scallops and keep cool. Heat Himalayan salt block in oven for 30 minutes at 400 F. Combine relish ingredients mix and reserve. In medium 2 qt heavy bottom sauce pot add sunflower seeds thru black pepper, simmer on low heat constantly stirring to avoid burning until risotto become thick about 20 minutes. Turn off heat, mix in Gruyere cheese and green onions and keep warm. Place salt block on gas burner on low heat. Sear scallops for 4 minutes per side, using a vegetable peeler make carrot peelings and place in ice water.

To plate appetizer, place 2 oz of risotto, top with one large scallop, top with 2 Tbs of relish garnish with lemon zests, thyme sprig, carrot shavings and micro greens.

Makes 4 Servings

Apple Benton Bacon BLT Bites

Presented by Chef Greg Eisele C.E.C. and 2016 Culinary Program Student Kimberly Denise Ault

2	fresh granny smith apples, julienned
2 Tbs	golden raisins, chopped fine
1 c	white balsamic vinegar
1 tsp	crushed red pepper
1 tsp	rosemary, fresh chopped
2 oz	honey
2 oz	leeks, thin julienne strips
4 strips	Benton Bacon
2 qt	fresh blueberry
2 c	white balsamic vinegar
1 Tbs	crushed red pepper
1 qt	extra virgin olive oil - Cold 40 F
12 oz	Roma tomato concasse
6 oz	water
2 Tbs	agur agur
12 oz	yellow tomato concasse

Combine apples through rosemary and simmer for 5 minutes. Cool. Place 4 each leek juliennes on bacon strips top with 3 each apple sticks, wrap and secure with toothpick. Simmer yellow tomato concasse with water and red tomato concasse with water, keep separate, add Agur Agur to both hot tomato mixtures and simmer for 5 minutes. Strain mixtures using a fine chinoise strainer. Drizzle tomato mixtures making large droplets into cold vegetable oil. Keep cold and reserve. Bake bacon wraps for 15 minutes at 350 F until crispy and golden brown.

Serve Bacon bites with Tomato Caviar and Micro greens.

Makes 4 servings

Boursin Crab Chimichanga with Mango Salsa

Presented by Chef Greg Eisele C.E.C. and 2016 Culinary Program Student, Rosaninia Sevillejo Foxworthy

Filling

6 oz	Boursin cheese
3 Tbs	celery small dice
2 Tbs	onion small dice
2 Tbs	red pepper roasted, small diced
1 Tbs	fresh dill
1 Tbs	lemon zests
1	egg white
1/4 c	panko bread crumbs
10 oz	shelled lump blue crab
	Flour spinach tortilla shell cut 4" x 6"

Mango Salsa

4 oz	tomato, diced
2 Tbs	cilantro, fine chopped
2 oz	yellow onion, diced
1 Tbs	jalapeno, seeded diced
2 oz	mango, skinned diced
1	lime, juiced

Gently fold and mix Boursin cheese through crab meat. Reserves keep cool. Steam tortilla shell, for 30 seconds over water bath. Portion 3 oz of crab mixture in tortilla shell and wrap burritos style. Cool. Mix tomatoes through fresh lime juice for the salsa. Saute chimichanga in coconut oil in medium saute pan until both side are golden brown and serve with mango salsa. Garnish with fresh cilantro, lime wedges and crab claws.

Makes 4 Servings

Like the original culinary dishes that one might create in his or her kitchen, this cookbook is a first-time effort for us. We have greatly learned from this endeavor, have had a ton of fun and look forward to improving on future editions. We sincerely appreciate your support and grace as you graze upon how we have attempted to share our passion (mistakes and all) with you as first-time, self-published authors.

We take great inspiration in this feat as we are reminded of the words shared by the late Master Chef Julia Childs when she reflected upon trial and error principles, "This is my invariable advice to people; Learn how to cook --try new recipes, learn from your mistakes, be fearless and above all have fun!"

We look forward to sharing our growth with you in both the culinary and written arts in the future. Until then, Bon Appetite!

Contributors

Jesse Johnson

Jesse Johnson has a passion for total wellness in all facets of life. With a B.A. in religion from Maryville College, he understands that complete wellness includes both physical and spiritual aspects. As a previously overweight teen, Jesse also understands the difficulties of battling bad habits and overcoming challenges while making long-lasting lifestyle changes. Jesse was born and raised in East Tennessee and has a passion to help those within the region. As a certified personal trainer and someone with a passion for nutrition, Jesse desires to assist others in both fitness and dietary guidance so that individuals can achieve their goals while living healthy, happy lives.

Jesse Johnson

Frank Bisek

A native Minnesotan, Frank moved to Knoxville two years ago with his partner Becca. He likes to be active and outdoors, including playing rugby for the Knoxville Possums. Frank is available for design and layout work. Looking for a logo for your business or an upcoming event? Need a new or updated website? Contact him at fbisek@gmail.com.

Frank Bisek

Elizabeth Myers

Elizabeth Myers is the co-owner of e2 photography with her husband, Eric and is a native of Knoxville, Tennessee. She has photographed everything from specialty cakes and family meals to serving as a regular contributing photographer in the University of Tennessee Culinary Program under the direction of Director Chef Greg Eisele. It was through him that she became acquainted with Michelle, Scott and the Totality Living Well team. Elizabeth's affiliation with culinary arts also includes food styling. As an artist in the fields of photography and architecture, Elizabeth's desire is to entice the viewer from her perspective. She has enjoyed working with Michelle, Scott, and the team during the production of this book and hopes that her images entice the readers of this book to try the recipes she has photographed.

Elizabeth Myers
e2 photography

Credits for photos on pages: 54, 58, 63, 65, 72, 93, 115, 128, 130, 133, 146, 157, 160 and 162

Colby McLemore

Colby McLemore of Colby's Photography is an award-winning international Master photographer based in Knoxville, TN. He focuses on advertising, commercial, business, and portrait photography. One of his favorite genres of product photography is food. He was thrilled to work with Michelle, Scott, and the rest of the team. One of the images he photographed while working with them won honors at the International Photographic Competition sponsored by the largest and oldest professional photographer's trade organization, Professional Photographer of America.

Colby McLemore
Colby's Photography

Credits for photos on pages: Cover, 22, 39, 40, 47, 48, 57, 68, 81, 85, 86, 86, 89, 96, 101, 105, 110, 118, 143, 154 and 158

39703285R00097

Made in the USA
Middletown, DE
23 January 2017